Reasons
To Believe

Fresh devotional insights

from the

Gospel of John

Graham Field

26; 08; 21. With Lots Of Love

To Stephen & Julie

From Mum Marks
x x x
x x

DEDICATION

To my wife Ann, thank you for doing the journey of life with me for over 40 years.

Introduction

My love for John's gospel began in university days. We needed to do a module on John. The tutor advised us that for the exam we needed to memorise the structure of the book off by heart. That more or less meant knowing the structure of 'sevens' that John used in his text. I found that so fascinating. Over the years I have discovered the 'sevens' can be arranged in different ways than the course book laid down, but I still remained fascinated. During a period of over 50 years of Christian ministry I have taught many times from the Gospel of John. Often this has been in the form of a series of teachings to different groups of people. I have used titles such as, 'I give you Jesus; It's all about Jesus; or simply The Gospel of John. In each case I wanted to convey the centrality of the person of Jesus in the thinking of John. Now that I am retired, I have the time to reflect on these endeavours and to see if these many years of study can be recorded permanently for the benefit of future generations. Each time I turned to the book it seemed as if fresh layers of meaning were released. This is my latest, and probably my last such endeavour.

I have chosen this time a new title, *Reasons to Believe*, because I wish to show the steps John and his companions took, from the man with the compelling aura they met on the shore of Galilee, to the confession that he was indeed God in human form. At each step they were confronted with astounding evidence that they had to process. Sometimes they got it and other times they had to backtrack and think it over. John takes us along with him on this odyssey by means of relating to us a selection of these experiences, in order that we too may believe.

John portrays a realistic honesty, in that, although he was facing the most momentous days in human history there were many who refused to believe what they had seen. Consequently, he deals with the nature of belief itself. To him it was not a matter of being bombarded into submission by the facts, but what was seen and heard required a spiritual enabling or enlightening, to grasp the significance of what was observed.

It is beyond the scope of my intention to go into great detail regarding the technical and literary peculiarities of the book. But some comments need to be made to support our ongoing understanding of the text.

Apart from the 'Prologue' and the 'Epilogue,' I have laid out the book according to the categories which are contained in the book. This means that it does not flow from verse to verse from beginning to end. However, it does emphasise the themes that impacted John as a result of his encounter with Jesus. This makes the book useful for devotions, bible study and sermon preparation. I have included a chapter and verse index for anyone who would like to read systematically.

The textual references from John are indicated by the numbers of the chapter and verse only. All other biblical books had the name of the book as well. The standard reference version is the NIV. All other references are identified at the place of quotation. When the text is directly quoted it is in italics. When it is paraphrased it is not. The New Testament and Old Testament are referred to as NT and OT respectfully.

I will concentrate on the author, what he saw and heard, how this impacted him, why he structured the work in the way that he did, and what he proposed to achieve through writing this gospel. This will mean, that to some extent, we will need to take a glimpse, into the mind of the author. So, we must identify him.

John makes it clear why he wrote the Gospel and what he hoped it would achieve. 20;30; 21:24,25.

These things are written that you may believe that Jesus is the Christ the Son of God. And that by believing you may have life in his name.

Everything we shall say in this book is based on this declared purpose. We shall see that the component narratives are not primarily about the people and the circumstances they illustrate, but they are primarily revealing to us who Jesus is so that we may believe.

Authorship and Date.

This Gospel appears in the New Testament at the head of the Johanine Corpus, a collection of documents all bearing the name Johannes or John. The other documents being the three letters of John and the book of Revelation. Researchers have questioned whether these works were produced by the same author.

The main problem that troubles most scholars it seems, arises from the quality of the Greek language in the text. The Letters and the Gospel are, apparently, very similar and are of a reasonably high standard of Greek. It is generally accepted that they were the work of one person. The book of Revelation shows an inferior grasp of Greek. The argument is, how can an unlearned Galilean fisherman be the author of such sophisticated Greek documents as the Gospel and the letters, and how could the writer of such good Greek be the author of Revelation in a grammar of inferior quality?

The objection that John was unlearned is based on Acts 4:13. We must ask if this was a statement of fact or the usual aspersion thrown at people from Galilee, an example from the same group of people is found in 7:50-52. Just because someone comes from a lowly background does not mean they are not intelligent and can develop learning given the right opportunity.

We must also note that although they may have been unlearned to the standards of the people speaking, the whole reason for the comment was that they were speaking with a fluidity and quality equal to that of learned men. This ability, the book of Acts tells us, comes from two sources, one they had been with Jesus and two they were filled with the Holy Spirit.

In addition to this we shall see that the documents of the Johanine corpus were written some thirty years after the events of which they spoke. That is plenty of time for a man to educate himself in the finer points of a language, especially if he found himself in exile on a remote island. We have seen in the founders of modern Pentecostalism in the early years of the 20th century, men of little academic learning, rise from the more menial levels of society to become theologians of remarkable ability. Often, they would eclipse those who had attained academic excellence. We attribute that to the work of the Holy Spirit.

Incidentally, the reason that the Greek in Revelation is substandard may be the same for all sections of sub-standard Greek in the New Testament. That is the particular sections were first written in Hebrew/Aramaic and then translated into Greek. [1]

John, or Johannes, was a fairly common name at the time of Jesus as its use in the NT would confirm. Orthodox researchers have noted a John Mark, a John the Evangelist, a John the Divine and a John the Elder as associates with the apostolic group. [2] There may have been such people but the 'John' we are looking for had to be present at the last supper. 21:20. It seems that the objections to the authorship of John son of Zebedee stands on more shaky ground than the traditional assumption.

Like the other gospels the book does not have an autograph. Unlike the other gospels however the author leaves cryptic clues as to who he may be without actually saying so. This is mainly in John 21: 20-24. The phrase used is *the disciple whom Jesus loved.'*

With this pseudonymity in mind, we can deduce the following; The author was a regular companion of Peter. Luke 22:8; Acts 3:1; Acts 8:14; Mark 14:33.

The author was sitting next to Jesus at the last supper. John 13: 23.

---

[1] **David Biven. Understanding the difficult words of Jesus.**

[2] **WWW. Bibleodyssey**

The author was very familiar with the features of the land of Israel and of Jerusalem in particular. John 5: 1-5.

The author was very aware of Jewish festivals and customs and their meaning. Luke 22:7.

One further thing that remains in the objections is found in 18:15-16. If the 'other disciple' is John, on what basis did he have access to the High Priests house? The answer is we do not know. But we must ask why was it not possible for John to have some means of access to the compound of the High Priest?

There is no reason to object that the author was John the son of Zebedee.

We may ask why the anonymity?

In relation to writing the gospels we can only assume that the author feels his life would be in danger should he be identified. Persecution of Christians was not always at a high and intense level and it was not the same in all areas of the empire. We can assume that the book was first written in a time of acute danger. Most traditions indicate that it was written in Ephesus.

He had to be anonymous, but not so anonymous that those in the know would not be able to recognise him. By a process of deduction, John is the only one of the inner circle of disciples that is not named in the Gospel of John.

Written evidence of authorship has a distinctive pedigree. One of John's disciples was a man called Polycarp of Smyrna. (60-155 ad.) He is quoted by a second century church father called Iranaeus, (130-202 ad.) also of Smyrna, as having written, that John told him of the writing of the gospel.

Polycrates (circa189 ad) Clement of Alexandria (circa 200 ad) and Eusebius (circa 300 ad) each authenticate that the evidence available to them confirmed John the son of Zebedee as the author of the fourth gospel. [3]

---

[3] **Jones. The Titus Institute**

Date.

In dating the Gospels, we must bear in mind that there is a difference between the original form of the documents and the way we see them today. Luke makes this clear in Luke 1:1-4. Luke was not an eye-witness so his Gospel was entirely based on pre-existing material or the testimony of eye-witnesses. It seems clear that some of this material was also available to Matthew and Mark to which was added personal recollections.

A critical event in dating the New Testament manuscripts is the destruction of the Temple and the City of Jerusalem in the year 70. Each of these Gospels must have been compiled into their final form before this date, because although they mention the destruction prophetically as a future event, they do not say that it had actually happened.

John also contains evidence of an evolution of the text. 7: 52-8:11 is understood to be an insertion. [4] Chapter 21 is clearly an addition. [5] That is not to say John didn't write them but they were not all written at the same time. As John lived into the 90's there was plenty of time for the text to evolve. We can say that these are the words of John, if not entirely the work of John

John 21:19 indicates that John knew of Peter's death when he wrote and that he himself had survived to an advanced age as the text suggested he would. It seems well established that Peter died under the persecution of Nero in or about 67. Jerusalem as John knew it, was destroyed in 70.

In all his detailed description of the city of Jerusalem there is never any hint that it was past tense. We must assume then that John wrote about the time of Peter's death before the destruction of Jerusalem. Maybe it was the death of Peter that triggered the desire to write. In this case a date would be

---

[4] **John Gospel of Belief. Tenney**
[5] **John Gospel of Belief. Tenney**

around 69. The dates that are most commonly accepted for the compilation of the Gospels indicate when they reached their final form, not when they were first written down.

One final thing about the dating is to note the 'Rylands Fragment.' This is a tiny scrap of parchment, found in Egypt, written in Greek, containing an extract from the Gospel. It is dated about 125. As a fragment, by definition, must be part of the whole, so it can be determined that the Gospel of John was circulated in its final form before this date.

The Structure of the Gospel.

John makes his intentions clear in 20:30-31; 21:24-25. He is telling a largely sequential story but is not strictly bound by chronology. The story of the clearing of the Temple 2:12-23 is an example of this. The other Gospels place this event near the end of Jesus' ministry. It would be difficult to conceive of this event happening twice, and so we conclude John placed it out of order for literary or theological purposes to achieve his goal of bringing people to belief. From chapter 7 onwards John's story is set in and around Jerusalem. Also, John deals with meaning and significance of the events he describes to a far greater extent than the other gospels. The teaching on the Holy Spirit is also unique to John.

He chose events that had impacted him personally on the basis that if they had brought him to belief and understanding they would have the same effect on others. Some of the accounts are held in common such as the feeding of the 5000 and the storm on the lake.

From the book of Acts, we can see that the early preaching of the Apostles and their companions comprised of telling the story of Jesus as the occasion demanded, showing its roots in the Hebrew Scriptures and applying a meaning that demanded action. On this basis we can be sure that John would tell the stories of his journey with Jesus over and over again, and as the stories were retold, more and more of the meaning of what had happened would become clear to him.

Matthew thought it important to authenticate the person of Jesus by means of recording the Messianic heritage. This, to him, was proof of the Messianic claims. Hence his gospel begins with the Abrahamic lineage.

Mark, the authentication was established when he began to preach. What he said and did were the only sources required to establish the authenticity of his claims. Mark begins with the public ministry of Jesus.

Luke felt that Jesus was authenticated through the details of his miraculous birth. The beginning for him was the amazing events that accompanied his birth.

John was convinced that the authenticity of Jesus' claims was found in who he was, the eternal Son of God who took on human form. The beginning for John was in eternity.

Reasons to Believe

CONTENTS

Textual Index

ACKNOWLEDGMENTS

I would like to express sincere thanks to Pastor John Caldwell for his patient advice and guidance regarding the layout, publishing, and printing of this book.
I would also like to thank Pastor John price for proof-reading the manuscript, his sound advice and constant encouragement in the work of the Lord.

CHAPTER 1.
THE PROLOGUE. 1: 1-28.

The prologue could really be seen as John's conclusion about who Jesus was. When he had considered all that he had seen and heard, and how it had impacted his life and the life of all those he had ministered to, he came to this profound conclusion. John then proceeds to give us the evidence that impacted him so that we also may believe. Throughout the Gospel we will see that we are being continually referred back to these opening statements.

Our title is, 'Reasons to Believe.' And so it is. This Gospel is to present to us, Jesus. All the signs, statements and encounters are revealing something more about the incredible person John knew, so that we may come to know him as well.

The Beginning.

John's gospel does not start with the story of Jesus' birth as Matthew and Luke do, or when he began to preach as Mark does. John feels it is important that we know that Jesus has come from the realms of God himself. The matter of where Jesus came from will have enormous implications as the story unfolds. Jesus was stepping into a world that John knew only too well. It was important who your father was, where you came from and what school you attended. Your origin would determine your status in society and the level of authority you could attain. John therefore begins with these unassailable words, *'In the Beginning.'*

The phrase immediately links us to the first verses of the Bible. *'In the Beginning God.....* It is the source of all authority and responsibility for all that was to be said and done. In the same way John opens with this pertinent phrase.

John was saying, as it were, "Everything I am about to tell you comes with the Divine Authority of Almighty God who brought all things into existence in the first place."

.

- Jesus was already there when the beginning of time emerged.
- Jesus shared in the creative acts of God.
- Jesus shared the essence of the life of God.
- Jesus was God.
- What was about to be told was equally a work of God as creation itself.

Now this is something to believe. Not something to learn or calculate. This is the way it is, embrace it, believe it and we are on our way to an encounter with the Son of God.

This is so important. The Gospel of Jesus Christ did not immerge from the turmoil of humanity. It came down from heaven. What we believe was not a result of man seeking God, but as a result of God seeking man.

It was not an enlightened man observing poverty, inequality, greed, anger, or disease and devising a system to alleviate the problem, but a loving God who penetrated the darkness of sin with the light of his presence, in order to show us the way into a relationship with him.

John calls Jesus, 'The Word,' the one who was to speak to us the words of God, demonstrates the works of God, reveal the heart of God, and include those who believe in the family of God.

We are all fairly familiar with fact that this word '*Word*' is a translation of a Greek philosophical term, '*the Logos.*' [6] As such it meant, reason, will, or intelligence. It came to mean in Greek philosophy 'The principle of Divine reason and Order.' In modern speech it could be substituted with the phrase, '*Intelligent Design.*' But the term did not only carry a Greek meaning, it carried a Hebrew meaning as well. The Hebrew word '*Debar,*' means to speak with authority and is the root word for 'commandments.' It was understood as a Name for God in certain Jewish traditions. [7] It is based on Numbers 7:89 where Moses entered the Tabernacle to speak with God and '*he heard a Voice Speaking to him from the mercy seat.*' In Hebrew it is, 'HaKol MiDebar' '*The voice who was speaking.*' Hence, far from this being a new expression it is a brilliant combination of a Greek term and a Hebrew term and both John's Greek and Hebrew audience would know exactly what he meant. [8]

John then proceeds to tell us what relationship this being called 'The Word' has with the following;

God;
'*with God*' He was at home in the sacred confines of the being of God, yet there was something, yet to be revealed, that granted him a personal distinction, by which he would come to be known.

'*was God*' He was in fact entirely indistinguishable from God, partaking of the same essential nature. Yet as we shall see, he could 'speak' to the Father, and 'send' the Holy Spirit as if they were separate beings. This is a mystery, upon which, the writings of John cast some considerable light.

---

[6]The Interlinear Greek English NT. Nestle.

[7] Abarim Publications.

[8] Hebrew English Bible. Society for the distribution of Hebrew scriptures.

What God said, he said. What God did, he did. God's will was, the same was his will.

Creation;

His creative acts brought all things into being. The potential of both good and evil emanated from His creative design, because it included free will. (Genesis 4:6) The Word was only subject to the forces of man and nature because he chose to be so. There was nothing that could compel him down a certain avenue. It would soon become clear that the Voice that stilled the wind and calmed the waves would also roll away a tombstone. Jesus said to Pilate, *'you would have no power over me if it were not given you from above. Therefore, the one who handed me over to you is guilty of the greater sin.' John 19:11.* Sin and evil will never muster enough force to overthrow Him because they are merely emanations of the creation. As we shall read in a moment, *'the world did not recognise him,'* but that ignorance did not diminish Him.

Life.

'His life was the Light of men.' His appearance, the way he related to God, religion, people, and the creative order was intended to be a light to show them what it was that God required of man. He shone into the darkness as the Light of creations dawn had shone into the darkness in the beginning. The light was to show the right path and the wrong path. The light was to reveal God as he really was, not as he had been obscured. This was no longer a set of commandments and list of rituals to which they were to attain. It was a 'Living Being' who walked before God as God desired man to walk.
But the darkness was so intense that many did not in any way comprehend what they were looking at.

World.

4

What 'world' was that? The planet earth, the rivers and the mountains? The people, both good and bad? The world as man had distorted it? What world was it that God loved? (3:16) The world He loved was the world he designed and the world as he intended it to be. So deep was his desire to bring about the world as it was designed that he provided a way where those who would believe in him could inhabit it.

His own.
Those with the same human ancestry as he had taken on. A people who, for a thousand years or more, had the words of the prophets before them, shining a light into their darkness. But they had become so accustomed to rejecting the prophets, they rejected him too.

He came to the Jew first because of God's promise to Abraham, that through his offspring the world would be blessed. Although John does not present to us an ancestry as do Matthew and Luke, by using the phrase 'his own,' we see he was fully aware of the relationship of Jesus to Abraham.

To those who received him.
The privilege of entering into the family of God was to be bestowed, not to those born of the right family, but to those who would believe. This is remarkable. John had seen what few others saw at the time, that the appearance of the 'Word' was for all people, not just the family of Abraham.

Humanity.
The Word became flesh. This is John's summary of the nativity story. That's all we need to know at this stage, God became man, he dwelt amongst us as one of us. He was born into the Hebrew world, as we have said, because God had made a covenant with the founder of the Hebrew nation, Abraham, that this Saviour would be of his family. He breathed our air, he walked our road, he ate our food, he felt our

feelings, he spoke our language, and he submitted to the physical limitation of time and space, he was not an illusion.

Only a few recognised him, only a few received him. But those that did believe realised that what they had seen was the presence of God and what they had heard was the voice of God.

No one through human effort, religious observance, or intellectual exercise has ever seen God. He remained beyond the reach of man. But when God decided to make himself known, we saw him in the person of Jesus. This is John's testimony.

Jesus stepped in to history but was unaffected by history. Jesus is not shaped by the prejudices and world views that history implants in the mind of ethnic groups and are passed on from generation to generation. In a few verses we will encounter the story of Jesus and the woman at the well. Social history had determined that the Jews had to keep separate from the Samaritans. Jesus demonstrated that he was above the prejudices of history when he asked for water.

Likewise in Matthew's pertinent account Matthew 15: 21-28, he showed that resentments and hatred that history had planted in men's hearts was of no hindrance to him.

His Glory.

Jesus stepped into a biological process but was not restricted by the frailty of humanity. Whatever genetical frailty was in the line of his mother, physical or mental, it did not affect him. He did not inherit anything mentally or physically that would affect his mission. He was not delusional, paranoid, or psychotic. He was born into poverty, raised in obscurity, was a refugee from ethnic cleansing, he lost his guardian-father at a relatively young age, yet none of these things distorted his feelings, thinking, or the way he viewed life. His heart and mind remained perfectly pure throughout. Even death was not inevitable to him as he declared, *'no one takes my life from me, I lay it down of myself.' 10:18.*

He brought the gospel down from heaven, which did not belong to, or emerge from any particular group. Even though the law of Moses came down from God. It is what his people had done with the law that Jesus opposed. The gospel is not something for an ethnic group, *'children born, not of natural descent'* but people birthed into the gospel by the will of God when they encountered Jesus. All they had to do was believe and so receive.

He came down from God, out of the beginning, the pure essential revelation of God. And John records that this is what he saw. 'The Glory of the One and Only to come to earth from heaven.'

The gospel is all about Jesus. The bible is important, church is important, ministries are important. But the power of God is released into our lives at the point when we believe who Jesus is.

The Contrast, Moses and Jesus.

The law revealed the Holiness of God and the sinfulness of man. Its sacrifices only stayed the hand of Divine judgement. If the sacrifices were not performed, then iniquity built up until it spilled over into judgement, plague, conquest and slavery. The law, of itself, does not know mercy, compassion or pardon. The law was a shadow of what was to come. In type, symbol and principle it gave a hazy picture of what was to come. But when the 'life' that was 'light' came we saw and heard something new. 'Grace and Truth.' Moses brought the law to the people. But he was not the law. Jesus on the other hand not only brought the Gospel. He was the Gospel. We saw Grace and Truth in action. 'We will shortly come across this issue, *'Moses says, what do you say?'* (8:5) Then we hear the remarkable words, *'neither do I condemn you, go and sin no more.'* It was not just saying, 'don't do it again,' but granting the woman the ability to rise above whatever had dragged her down so that she would never return to what she was. This truth had never been made known before. In this way God was made known to us.

John the Baptizer.

Remember at this time, John, the son of Zebedee was a disciple of John the Baptizer.

We are now introduced to him. He was also sent from God, but not in the same way as Jesus was. '*I am the Voice.*' He was also a 'Voice' a '*Debar*' 1:23 But he was a Voice of a different order.

Are you the Christ? No.

Are you Elijah? No.

Are you that prophet? No.

Then who are you?

He was merely a Voice, but what a voice. He was putting sounds to the words of God.

John the Baptizer was the last in the long line of Prophets who had brought the word of the Lord to the Hebrew people. Jesus was to call him the 'Greatest of them all.' Matthew 11:12-16.

John was the greatest for the following reasons;

- He was the last. In him welled up all that had been said before from Abraham to Malachi.
- He knew the ultimate revelation, the identity of the Messiah. Isaiah had seen his suffering, Micah, his place of birth, but John knew who he was.

He came as a witness to the Light. He was not the Light; he was its witness. John's preaching must have been profound because of the way he was questioned. It is clear that it was thought he was the Messiah and they came to him to confirm it, but he would not. So great was John's impact that some 30 years later Paul found a group of believers in Ephesus, who it seems, upheld John as the Messiah. Acts 19:1-5.

John operated from the east of the river Jordan, in the wilderness, technically outside of the Land of Israel. There he baptised. How did he do that? He would probably have led people down into the water. Seen that they were fully immersed and then rose again out of the water on the other side of the river, in the Land of Israel. How do we know this? Well, there are four things that suggest it.

- This place is traditionally believed to be the place where Elisha crossed the river after the ascension of Elijah. Miraculously the waters parted and he crossed back into the Land of Israel to commence his ministry. It was then said the Spirit of Elijah is resting on Elisha. (2 Kings 6-15.)
- It is also believed to be the place where Joshua miraculously crossed the river when he brought the descendants of Jacob into the land promised to Abraham. (Joshua 3:5-17)
- In Jewish ritual baptisms it was the custom to enter the water along one pathway or staircase and to leave by another. One was the unclean and the other the clean.
- When Jesus was baptised and came up out of the water Luke tells us he 'returned' from the Jordan. (Luke 4:1) He had crossed back from East to West and was now in the land of His ministry. John tells us Jesus begins his ministry the next day. Jesus did not need to repent, but he walked the way of those who did, because 'he was numbered with the transgressors.'

John's baptism was a baptism of repentance. The people were challenged to leave the land, repent of their hypocrisy and re-enter the land with renewed zeal to do the will of God. It's all about Jesus. John the son of Zebedee is telling us that everything that had gone before was pointing to one person. All prophecy up to this moment had been honed, as it were, into the point of a spear. John took that spear and hurled it into the future. One greater than John the Baptizer was about to appear. John the baptizer would know who he was because God had told him he would see the Holy Spirit in the form of a dove come upon him. When he saw this, he would know that the new era had begun. This was the Messiah of Israel, Jesus the Christ, the Saviour of the World.

It seems shortly after this John was imprisoned and eventually executed.

This is the considered Christology of John. He was fully God. He by nature possessed all that God possessed. Yet he also appeared as a man. But not as a great man, or a powerful man, but as a lowly man, a servant. As Paul was later to put it, *'being in the very nature of God, he did not consider equality with God something to be grasped. But made himself nothing, taking the very nature of a servant.* Philippians 2:6-7. On the one hand we beheld his glory and on the other we beheld his poverty. He walked through the waters of repentance with the sinners so that His grace would not miss anyone. This is the Jesus John knew. This is the 'Jesus' he asks us to believe in.

CHAPTER 2.
THE FIRST TO BELIEVE. 1: 19-51

In this next section John tells us how he and five other individuals came to believe in Jesus and set out on their journey of Faith. It is incredible for us to look at this. We are familiar with accounts and stories of great evangelical events, where people like John Wesley, George Whitfield, George Jeffries, Billy Graham, Reinhard Bonnke and many others brought hundreds of thousands of people to Faith in Jesus, sometimes many thousands at one event. Here are the first six, one or two at a time. Here is how it happened and this is what has happened multiple millions of times since.

John the Baptizer. 1:29-34.
We have already clearly stated that John was the greatest of the prophets. He laid a spiritual foundation on which Jesus was to launch his ministry. Being such a man of God, John knew that his work was transitionary. There was one coming after him who would accomplish the plan of world redemption. *'Among you stand one you do not know. He is the one who will come after me, the thongs of whose sandals I am not worthy to untie.'* 1:26-27.

How did John come to believe? *'I saw the spirit come down from heaven as a dove and remain on him. I would not have known him except the one who sent me to baptise told me, 'The man on whom you see the Spirit come down is he who will baptise with the Holy Spirit. I have seen and testify that this is the Son of God.'* 1:32-34.

John believed because of a prior divine encounter. God had said to him when you see a certain sequence of event unfold, then, that is the One. Many have come to know Jesus because of a supernatural encounter that God had prepared them for. This doesn't happen to everyone. It is when a certain sequence of events unfolds and you find someone is giving you answers to questions only God knows you have asked. It is as if your deepest thoughts have been spoken back to you. This is what people full of the Holy Spirit can do. They are not aware of the significance of what they have said or done until the event occurs, this is something that God has put together so that people may believe.

Behold the Lamb of God.
This phrase 'Lamb of God' is virtually unique to John writings. The only other place where a similar term is used directly of Jesus is in Revelation. This is an indication that the two books are by the same original author. Paul and Peter make descriptive references to Jesus as the Lamb. Why did John the Baptizer say this?
The imagery of the Lamb is drenched in Hebrew symbolism and is entirely associated with sacrifice. So much so that the words could be interchanged. John could have said 'Behold God's Sacrifice to take away the sin of the world.'
Imagine our author watching and listening to this. Two men on a spiritual level, which at that time, John could never fathom, speaking of the mystery of the plan of world redemption.
We note that when Jesus began to speak in more detail of his impending death, it was Peter who objected. John remained silent. Peter had not heard these words John had.
We shall see that Peter and a significant number of the twelve were convinced Jesus was the Messiah and understood the

implications of setting Israel free from Rome and establishing the kingdom of which the prophets spoke. What was almost impossible for them grasp was, the suffering Messiah. But as John looks back over the years, he recalls that it was clear from the beginning, it was the mandate from God delivered by John the Baptizer, *'The Lamb of God.'*

I have already described how all the weight of biblical prophecy up to this point welled up in the heart of John. Paramount in that plethora of divine utterances was the matter of the Suffering Messiah.

Abraham, prophesied; *'God will provide the lamb.'* Genesis 22:8

Isaiah declared, *'he was led like a lamb to the slaughter and as a sheep before her shearers is dumb, so he did not open his mouth.'* Isaiah 53: 7. John with outstretched finger pointed to Jesus and said, *'Behold the lamb of God.'*

That takes way the sin of the world.
There is an aspect of sin that is common to all people. All sin is not common to all people. For example, a person may steal but not tell lies. Another person may tell lies but not steal. Those are sins but are not common to all. The sin of the world is the state into which we are born. Sin entered the world at the beginning through Adam aligning himself with God's enemy rather than God. God had invested in Adam the power to determine the spiritual state of succeeding generations. If he chose obedience then his descendants would be in relationship with God from birth. But he chose disobedience and so he was banished from God's presence and we are all born separated from God. (Isaiah 59:1-2; Ephesians 2:11-13.) This is what all people of the world have in common as far as sin is concerned. (Romans 5:12-17.)

As a result of this separation mankind has fallen under the influence of God's enemy, Satan, and that state of affairs means we have a tendency to promulgate the disobedience in personal acts of transgression. Sin then becomes an individual act as we have just mentioned.

Adam had done something that affected us all, Jesus came to do something else that would affect everyone. To remove the barrier that separated man and God. He did this first of all by atoning through his death for Adam's sin. This enabled mankind to hear the gospel of redemption, have the ability to believe it and so experience the presence of God once again. (1Corithans 15: 20-24) Then when someone actually, personally, believed in what Jesus had done, his sacrifice also atones for the individual sins that person had committed. As a result, as we shall see shortly, they will then be 'born again.' Someone who refuses to believe will remain condemned.

When Jesus was baptised, it symbolised that he was passing through the water on behalf of all humanity. When he rose from the water it symbolised that all humanity could potentially believe and receive eternal life.

When we pass through the water of baptism, it symbolises we are dying to the state in which we were born and rising to this new relationship with God that Jesus made possible. (Romans 6:1-4.)

In the Old Testament system of sacrifice two sacrifices are pertinent here. The sin offering and trespass offering. We find them described in Leviticus 4 and 5. The sin offering was to atone for the separation that Adam's transgression had brought about and temporally maintained a relationship with God for a specific period of time. Then it was repeated. The trespass offering did the same for individual sins and maintained a relationship with God until the person sinned again, then another sacrifice was required.

The Lamb of God came to deal with sin and trespass in one tumultuous spiritual encounter through his death and resurrection. In this way he took away the sin of the world.

He will baptise you with the Holy Spirit.

14

This statement comes without precedent. It tells us that Jesus will cause us to be immersed in something of the Essential Nature of God, the Holy Spirit. This baptism will enable us to maintain the new relationship we have entered into. We have learned from the Old Testament narratives that the Holy Spirit of God was a supernatural presence that enveloped certain individuals on specific occasions and enabled them to do phenomenal works of Grace and Power. The Holy Spirit at this time rested only on John and Jesus but was soon to be poured out on all who would receive him.

With all this welling up in his heart John the Baptizer bows out of the scene with these words, *'I have seen and testify that this is the son of God.'* (1:34)

Andrew and John the sons of Zebedee. 1:35-39.

We believe the other disciple to be John on the basis of our understanding of the unnamed disciple as explained earlier.

How did they come to believe? No supernatural encounter here. They went to where Jesus was staying and spent all day questioning him. We don't know what they asked but when the day was done their questions were exhausted, their doubts, fears, and scepticism was crushed, they believed. This is another pathway to Jesus. Many today have questions. Questions because of personal history. We can hear many things that claim to be the truth; we can hear many things about the failure of so-called Christians; we can hear of the claims of many different religions. We can ask our questions, but when God answers, we need to be ready to believe. I guess it was not the cleverness of the answers but the conviction that they sat in the presence of the One who had come from God. Two things are essential here. The questions must be honest enquiries, and the answers must be given in such a way that they present the presence of Jesus not just a superior knowledge.

They were convinced they had found the Messiah.

Simon Peter. 1:40-42

Simon came to believe because Andrew said to him. 'You have just got to meet the man I met yesterday' Andrew was different, he had changed. Simon had to meet this man. This is how Simon came to believe. He was so taken aback by the enthusiasm and passion of his brother; he knew something phenomenal had happened. This must be the most effective way of telling people about Jesus. One person who has met with Jesus conveying that experience to another. Many have come to faith by taking this journey. Finding Faith through someone who has found Faith.

Jesus changes his name. Jesus gave Simon a new identity. He had doubtless a reputation through his name Simon. Jesus was saying, we are starting again. I will call you 'Kephas,' which means 'rock.' That will better suit the work that you are going to do. Simon believed because Jesus released him from his past and he was aware something had happened. He would stumble and fall and right at the end of the book Jesus calls him Simon again. It was a re-launch from the denial.

Philip.1:43.

Now Philip's experience was different again. Jesus found Philip. Can you image it? Jesus, all the way from heaven goes to Galilee and searches until he finds one particular man, and says to him, 'follow me.' Alone, shy, introvert, maybe emotionally lost, apart from the crowd; he would never have found Jesus in a hundred years, he wasn't that type of person. So, Jesus found him. As this understanding dawned on Philip, he realised the significance of what was happening to him and so he believed. This is the testimony of many. It's another route to Jesus. People had no stirring for religion, God, or church, but then there is a dramatic encounter. This was Paul of Tarsus' experience in Acts 9. He was not just hiding away; he was working against the gospel. But he met with Jesus. Paul would never have come to Jesus so Jesus came to him.

It is interesting to note that Philip was the only one who Jesus personally chose.

Nathaniel. 1:45-50.
The sixth in the list of the first people who came to believe was Nathaniel. Now Nathaniel was someone else who had to be 'found.' Philip went to find him. Philip comes with all the enthusiasm of someone who has just met Jesus. 'We have found the one of whom the prophets spoke, it's Jesus of Nazareth.' Boom. The lead balloon landed. 'Can any good thing come out of Nazareth? Undaunted Philip carried on, if you don't believe me come and see for yourself. As soon as Jesus saw Nathaniel Jesus told him three things that no one else knew, except Nathaniel and God.
•   The desire and passion of your heart is to know more about God.
•   You were sitting under a fig tree when Philip found you.
•   You were thinking about how Jacob encountered God when he saw the vision of the ladder reaching to heaven.
    'Rabbi you are the Son of God the King of Israel.' Nathaniel believed because Jesus told him what Nathaniel knew only God knew. Therefore, he reasoned if this man knows what only God knows, he must be God. God works in the same way today; God is saying things to us that we have never told anyone. Why is he doing that. So that you may believe.
This is the witness of the first 6 men who came to believe. The man who walked our dusty road, hitched a ride in our fishing boat, sat down and ate at our table, and knew us better than we knew ourselves, was none other than Jesus of Nazareth, the Son of God, the Saviour of the world.
Life's journey may have brought us to a moment of encounter with Jesus. Maybe you can see yourself in the shoes of one of these six men, or maybe your journey is completely different. As you come under the words of the gospel you, like Nathaniel, are hearing things that only you and God knew.

This is happening because God is showing that he knows our heart. It is time to believe.

Jesus is the one without beginning. Forever he has been 'with God. There is nothing he cannot do because 'all things were made by him.' And there is nothing he does not know, 'for in him was light and his light was the light of men.'

CHAPTER 3.
SEVEN MIRACULOUS SIGNS

We have set a time for the original writing of the Gospel as some 30 years after the event. We have noted also that the basis of John's ministry over those 30 years would have been the telling and retelling of his journey with Jesus, what it meant to him, and what it brought him to believe about Jesus. From that plethora of information, which by John's own confession, would have filled the libraries of the world, he selected events that had significantly impacted him. His reasoning would have been, that if these things impacted him then they would impact others. So, they were recorded with the sole purpose of bringing generations who had not seen what he had seen, to the same experience of faith that he had enjoyed.

1. The Wedding at Cana. 2:1-11.

This the first of the Miraculous Signs that Jesus performed so that those who witnessed the sign, and, later, those who read about the signs would believe. It seems to be, not only the first of John's selection, but the first in order of the things Jesus did. 2:11.
I have often thought that if I were writing a Gospel as John was, what story would I have chosen as the first?
Restoration of sight to the blind; raising of a dead person to life? Something really attention grabbing and dramatic maybe.

When you think of it, on the surface, supplying extra wine to a wedding feast in an insignificant dusty village in the Galilean Hills, does not seem pertinent to revealing the Saviour of the World.

Yet the result of what he did at Cana was that he revealed his glory and his disciples believed on him. That is the 'glory' or renown, that he, as the one and only to come from God to man possessed. What in fact did he reveal?

Jesus revealed that he was Lord over human shortcomings.

When the collective wisdom of those who planned this wedding was put into action it was found that they had fallen short. There was insufficient wine. All the effort that had gone into the occasion was insufficient, man was exhausted and the whole scenario was about to collapse in chaos.

When human effort is exhausted, Jesus is only just beginning. We must be careful not to liken a wedding so long ago with what we are familiar with today. Both the wine and the water, or rather the lack of both was very important. It is difficult to specify exactly what was happening in this wedding as there was not just a single custom for weddings in Israel at the time. What can be said is that celebrations lasted over several days and that the wine and the water were used at intervals for significant rituals.

The lack of the wine meant that the rituals were also hampered.

The mother of Jesus involves him in the dilemma by pointing out that there is no more wine. Now Mary, (unnamed in John's Gospel) knew full well who Jesus was and at least something of what he was about to do. (Luke 1:26) She also knew that in presenting him with this problem he had the ability to solve it.

"Woman, why do you involve me, my time has not yet come.'

This sounds unnecessarily curt and dismissive to our western ears. But it is not so.

'Woman.' A term of tenderness and respect.

Why do you involve me? Why should you and I be involved in this situation? That's not an objection it's a search for faith.

Let us look at another woman in great need whom Jesus seemed to ignore. Matthew 15:21-27. The conversation seems unnecessarily harsh until we see what Jesus was looking for was a manifestation of faith, 'even the dogs eat the crumbs.'

It is the same here. Why should we be involved? Not 'why' I can't be bothered. But 'why;' what is the motivation in your heart behind your request?

The one answer could be, 'So that you can show off to the family.' The other and most likely answer would be 'to demonstrate the reason why you came.'

My time has not yet come. That is the time to openly manifest who he was, because to do that would also set in motion the pathway to the cross.

I see what happened next as Mary turning away from Jesus, maybe with a little swirl of her gown, with a secret smile on her face that only a mother and son could exchange, and say nonchalantly to the servants, 'just do what he says.' In this she revealed her belief in the authority he possessed. This is not too different from the next miraculous sign we shall look at shortly where the nobleman declared his faith in the authority of Jesus words. To put it another way, Jesus could solve this problem, demonstrate God's Glory, and yet not make it a public declaration of who he was.

So, the miracle was performed and only the disciples and few servants knew what had happened. This is similar to the story in Luke 5:12-15. Jesus asked for the miracle to be kept quiet because of the adverse repercussions it would stir up among the Jewish leaders.

Sometimes the Grace of God causes things to happen before their time. We must learn not to shout everything from the roof-tops as soon as it happens. Mary herself learned this lesson. Luke 2:51. The right time will come.

The disciples understood it, and their belief was strengthened, and that was all that was necessary for the time being.
Some versions describe this as the 'Beginning of Miracles.' Indeed, it was, it was the beginning of an age when the glory of a Kingdom yet to come can be known in part today.

Not only had the wine run out, but all it symbolised had run out as well. Israel was appointed to be light to the world directing people to God, but it had become pre-occupied with minutiae of its laws, the corruption of its sacrifices, and the exclusion of everyone but themselves, that few were finding God anymore.
We can be encouraged by this when someone who has come to the end of the road, or the edge of a cliff, or the bottom of the barrel, however best describes things. This is Jesus who comes when we have nothing more to give. He is Lord when we have come to the end.
When Jesus takes over the situation, like the wine at the wedding, it was better than it was before. The work of Jesus is a work of Quality. It's not a patching up. It's not a 'that will do for now.' It's not a band-aid or even a plaster-cast. It's a new beginning of the highest quality. They put water into the barrels, they drew water out, but they remained obedient. When the Master tasted it, it had become quality wine.

Jesus is the one who has the answer when the questions have run out.
Jesus is the one who gives value when the money has run out.
Jesus is the one who takes the broken, tired and weary, and gives it a brand-new start.
Jesus is the one who turns the end into the beginning.
Jesus is the one who takes the empty jars of failure, depression, despair and distress and fills them afresh with hope, purpose, and joy.

Jesus is the one who solved this problem and the person who failed was not exposed, and the majority of the people never knew there was anything wrong. The miracle blessed those who failed and those who had not. This reveals the glory of the Gospel and the wonder of the Grace of God.

So, Jesus revealed his glory. They saw through the scene of people, bride and groom, servants, empty jars, human failure. They saw Jesus the Son of God, and they understood what they had seen, and they believed. They picked up the compassion, the authority, the motivation, and the necessary obedience to the Son of God.
As John wrote down these words, I wonder, if he smiled to himself and said, 'I wonder if they ever found out where the wine came from.'

2. The Healing of the Nobleman's Son. 4:43-54.

This is the second of the seven miraculous signs. What is probably called in your bible the 'Healing of the Official's son.' The end of the story tells us the goal was once again achieved. The man and his household believed. 4:53. We can remind ourselves that this was the purpose that John wrote what he did; that we may believe. What did Jesus reveal about himself in this Miraculous Sign?

Here we see Jesus as the Lord over Space or Distance.
Jesus returned to the province of Galilee where a report of miracles performed in Jerusalem had preceded him. He went back to Cana. Here he pointed out 'a prophet has no honour in his own country.' Linking this to Matthew 13:53-58 and Mark 6:1-6 we can see that even His power to heal has something to do with the reception he received. His power to heal was effective only when he was honoured for who he was, a prophet, a man sent from God. A deeper understanding of

who he was would come in time, but for now, for those who knew no better, the honour of a prophet would do.

The word 'honour' has to do with Him as a person and is to be distinguished from applause or admiration for what he can do. At Cana Jesus meets a royal official. No doubt this man had come because he had heard about the previous sign, or even he had been there to witness it. He had a son who was terminally ill. He said to Jesus come to my house and heal him.

Jesus' response reveals the importance of the finer point we have just mentioned. There was plenty of applause in Galilee but not much honour.

Jesus saw and heard in this man's heartfelt cry that there was belief, at least to some degree, in who he was. 'Sir, come to my house before my child dies.'

Jesus detected the 'honouring' in his appeal.

The boy was in Capernaum, a journey of over 20 miles by foot. This story is very pertinent to us who have not seen but believed. Everything we do in church is based on the truth this story reveals to us. Jesus does not have to be physically present in order to perform a miracle. If the power of his word can span 20 miles, why not 200 or 2000 miles. Why not all the way from his throne in heaven to the need of an individual anywhere in the world today. He is Lord over space and distance. A similar miracle is recorded in Matthew 7:5-13. Once again, who Jesus is, and the authority he carries, is recognised by the centurion. That was the essence of his Great Faith.

From this we can learn; we do not have to be in a specific place, we do not have to be in a certain state of mind; we do not have to be doing religious things. We just have to honour Jesus for who he is. His word is sufficient to span distance and heal as if he was standing right there.

From where I live there is a fully functional hospital 5 miles away. There is another 3 miles away, and another 6 miles away. But if I am ill at home there is one big problem. Distance. But not with Jesus. His word is enough.

There are distances that cannot be described in miles. In a damaged relationship a couple can be described as being miles apart, but they are sitting next to each other. Emotional distance, spiritual distance. Today there are one's who can see themselves as being far from God. Lost, unseen, neglected, abused, under-valued; under a mountain of things that have been said and done that should never have been said or done. The miracle working words of Jesus span emotional and spiritual distance as well as physical distance. Here we begin understand what John meant when he called Jesus 'The Word.' The 'Word' that addressed the vast expanse of nothing and spoke all things into being, took on a human form and continued to speak. Words with such authority nothing can stand against them, words with force they can penetrate space and arrive at their destination as clear as they were said in the first place. *'Your son will live.'*

The miracle preceded the man home. When he got there, it was long done and dusted. He was healed at the moment Jesus spoke.

There was no applause when Jesus spoke. There was nothing to observe. But the man held an unwavering faith in who he was and that he had the authority to say what he said. The miracle arrived before the man. It is like when we have to face a situation we are dreading. Maybe called to a manager's office, called by a bank manager; called by a surgeon; certain that what we are about to hear is not good. Only to find when we got there it wasn't what we imagined at all. Time and again I have walked a rough road, dreading its conclusion. Only to find when I got to the end God had been there before me, the miracle had arrived before I did, and it was all sorted.

3. The Healing at Bethesda. 5:1-28

We are now back in Jerusalem. We have come to the third of the Miraculous Signs John chose to reveal to us who Jesus is. We probably call it 'The Healing of the paraplegic man at the Pool of Bethesda.' We are told that he had been a paraplegic for 38 years.

What it reveals to us is that Jesus is Lord over the passing of time.

This man had been an invalid for 38 years, not that he had been lying at the pool for 38 years, this may have been the first day he was there for all we know. But time had taken its toll on him. We detect a despair or resignation in his voice. We have noted that as John is giving us a selection of the miraculous signs that he saw Jesus perform, and he chose the one's that impacted him the most.

The Pool

Bethesda (House of mercy) was a real place; its remains are still there to see, just inside the Lion Gate of the Old City of Jerusalem. It was only after the unification of Jerusalem in 1967 that extensive excavations were carried out there and the remains of Bethesda were identified and the five-porched edifice was exposed. The fact that John can describe this place, which by the time the gospel reached its final form, was just a pile of rubble, proves his eyewitness credentials.

However, what went on in Bethesda is a little more intriguing. Some of the older versions of the Gospel contain the explanation that an angel disturbed the water periodically. That gave the water healing properties that would cure the first one who managed to get in. (5:4 KJV) Verse 7 tells us the waters were periodically disturbed. A verse 4 was inserted to give this an explanation. More recent versions omit verse 4. The oldest versions that exist of this passage do not contain the explanation. Only later versions have it. It is probably a marginal note that in the course of copying found its way into the text. [9]

The main reason why I think it is right to omit verse 4 is that it contradicts what we have come to know about God's grace. To only grant healing to the first in the water creates a sort of competition, where the fittest, or those with most help take the advantage of the healing. Jesus demonstrated the nature of Grace by going to the least able, those who could not help themselves, and grant them the miracle of healing.

Archaeology strongly suggests that there were two pools, one that gathered water from a spring and then fed the other. [10] This would be the case as many people bathing in the water would dirty it and it would need refreshing from time to time. This gives us the picture of the 'disturbed' water. It also follows that to get into the fresh water was better than getting into the dirty water. All mineral-saturated water has some therapeutic properties.

There was certainly a belief that the waters had healing properties as large numbers of people were brought there. But whether that belief was justified is improbable. Not everyone was brought there. The bible tells us of several people in Jerusalem who were blind or physically incapacitated at that time, who never went to Bethesda. Most notable is the story of the lame man healed through Peter and John in Acts 3. We are told that he had been taken daily for over 40 years to the entrance to the temple to beg for money. He was never taken to Bethesda.

It seems that Bethesda was originally a Jewish ritual bath, but by the first century the archaeology suggests it was a pagan shrine to Aesculapius, the Roman God of healing. [11] It would

---

[9] **Milne. The Message of John**

[10] **Biblical Archaeology Society**

[11] **Israel Institute of Biblical Studies**

indicate to us that Bethesda was a place of desperation, of last resort, and its reputation was believed in some circles but not others. It clearly was, at this time, not a Jewish shrine as it was operating on the Sabbath and the Jewish leaders were policing it as we can see. The man was accosted as soon as he stepped outside.

This would help understand the strange question from Jesus, 'Do you want to get well?' In other words, 'If you want to be well, what are you doing here?'

Time can be a problem. Especially if time is filled with pain, disappointment, rejection, inability, or embarrassment. The paralysis of the legs becomes a disease of the mind. Maybe he had been knocked down by a speeding chariot, in which case it was the drivers' fault; maybe he had been accidentally dropped by his mother, then it would be her fault; or maybe he was born that way, that makes it God's fault. We don't know but things like this would have haunted him. Our experiences in life can tell us that he was certainly gripped by despair, if not anger and resentment as well. So, he ended up at Bethesda, alone and abandoned.

Time can deal a series of painful and soul-destroying events. People can have travelled so long on this downward journey that they have lost all hope of a solution. This is the way it will be until I die. Nothing will ever change. Many have lived their life without much thought about God or Jesus or the bible. The years have rolled by. Even if there have been thoughts, like, there must be more to this than eat sleep and work, minds do not turn to Jesus. He is a remains a stranger, God and man are not on speaking terms.

Then there are people who have tried many things. Programmes and rituals, religions, fortune telling or spiritism, counsellors and advisors; yet they still carry a heavy burden around that is slowly crushing them.

This story reveals Jesus as Lord Over Time.

Why Jesus went to Bethesda we are not told. Why he went to this one man and not all the others, remains unexplained. But the sign that John saw that he thought we should know about was revealing Jesus as the Lord over time. He found a victim of time and instantly turning back the years so he could walk again. That is what he wanted us to see. Length of time does not cut us off from the power of God. Whatever time has driven us to do or believe it has not taken us beyond the reach of God.

It does matter how long God has been out of our lives, or even if he has never been in our lives, or where we have ended up. Jesus is passing our way. He didn't ask to be healed probably because he didn't think he could be healed. Maybe he thought the waters would help him. Jesus just strode into this scene of desperation and said to him, 'Stand up, pick up your bed, and walk.' And he was healed. Once again, the authority of the Words of Jesus rings out the testimony, 'This the Son of God.'

Do you want to be well? Let's ask the question another way. What will we allow God to do in our lives? It seems that he would have happy for Jesus to pick him up and put him in water. But what he got was a life transformation. *'Sin no more lest a worse thing come on you.'* Accumulated sin that crushed you becomes a platform to testify of the Saviours saving grace.

It wasn't the end of the matter. Jesus went to find him later on. He found him in the temple. As a lame man he would not have been allowed into the temple area. But now he could enter. It suggests he was showing his gratitude to God. Jesus' parting words were, *'see you are well gain, stop sinning or something worse may happen to you.'*

He then told the Jewish leaders that it was Jesus who made him well. Amazingly this brought about persecution for the man and the launching of plans to kill Jesus.

The Sabbath.

The point of contention is the supposed desecration of the Sabbath. The keeping of the Sabbath had virtually become a worship of the Sabbath. Apparently, there were 39 specific laws that were in place to protect the Sabbath from human violation.[12]

The Sabbath law was, that all work was to cease on this day. Deuteronomy 5:13-15.

You will notice we are still on the subject of time. This man had lived with his ailment through 1,976 sabbaths. Throughout this time successive Jewish leaders had made sure they never walked too far, never lifted a load, never lit a fire and never did any work on the Sabbath. But never once did they, or anyone else, reach out in compassion to this man, or any other man for that matter, because to so would violate the Sabbath.

The violation of the Sabbath was a point of contention which is covered in all of the Gospels. It does seem that Jesus deliberately healed on the Sabbath to provoke the debate and thereby reveal more of who he was.

'My Father is always at work to this very day, and, I too am working.' 5:17.

It is helpful for us to see some of the things that Jesus said as recorded in the other Gospels.

Matthew 12: 2-7. Jesus reminds them of two incidents where the sabbath was violated but it did not break the law. And ends with the statement, 'The Son of Man is the Lord of the Sabbath.'

Matthew 12:11. Jesus quotes a law which says that if an animal is distressed on the Sabbath, it is lawful to help it. He extrapolates this to conclude, 'therefore it is lawful to good on the Sabbath.

---

[12] *Chabad.org

Mark 2:27. In recounting the incident mentioned above, Mark adds the words, *'the Sabbath was made for man, not man for the Sabbath.'*

Luke 13:10-17. Here Jesus referred again to the practice of caring for animals on the sabbath, and implies how much more should we care for one another. He sees this woman as being bound by Satan and being freed on the Sabbath. Here it was suggested to Jesus that he should only heal on the other 6 days as it was work.

His response to these confrontations can be summed up in the theme of this passage. Jesus is Lord over time.

The sabbath was established for two purposes. Surprisingly, neither was a day of worship. The one was to rest and reflect on creation, that God was the Creator and provider of all things. The other was to reflect on the age that was about to come, the days of the Holy Spirit, which reflected in part the nature of the final Kingdom. Hebrews 2:2-4; 4:1-11.

In that Kingdom to come, the eyes of the blind will be opened, the ears of the deaf be unstopped the lame man would leap as a deer and the tongue of the mute shout for joy. Isaiah 33: 24; 35:5-6. It was to focus on the perfect world that was at the beginning and the perfect world that would come again.

Jesus healed and cast out evil spirits on the Sabbath day to demonstrate that the preaching of the Gospel would bring in part the power and virtues of that final Kingdom into people's lives through the power of the Holy Spirit. Hebrews 4:1-13. He showed that the Sabbath represented the perfect earth, without decay or sin, so as Lord of the Sabbath, he could perform works on the Sabbath, that reflected that perfect state. Furthermore, he was showing that everyone should be free to perform works of compassion, grace and mercy on the Sabbath, in order to relieve suffering and privation, to show the essential nature of the age to come.

The Sabbath was made for man, not man for the Sabbath. The state in which the people found themselves in the imperfect world is incompatible with properly observing the Sabbath because the Sabbath belongs to the perfect world. There will always be a sheep that falls into a pit, a blind man that needs guiding, a person oppressed by an evil spirit that needs delivering, and in John's story a lame man that needs healing. The Sabbath therefore, above all other days, is a day to relieve suffering because it points in part to that day when his Kingdom will come on earth. Jesus went to Bethesda, the 'House of Mercy', to perform an act of mercy and to announce that the Kingdom of God was encroaching in on the kingdoms of this world.

From now on all time is redemptive time because the Father is always at work.

The Father and the Son.

The fact that Jesus was calling God his Father was not lost on the Jewish leaders. They understood its implications, namely, he was equal to God. But instead of grasping the truth that God in his mercy had appeared in human form, they assumed that a man was falsely claiming to be God.

Here John expands on the opening comments of the Gospel, 'He was God.'

The actions are the same: what the Father does the Son does. The emotions are the same, whom the Father loves the Son loves. The judgements are the same; what the Father sees as right the Son sees as right. Their essential life force and authority is the same. Jesus was saying that he cannot help but heal on the Sabbath because that is what the Father designed it for, to bring into focus the world to come.

Once again, we find that word 'honour' in the text. 5:23. It calls us to look through and beyond the circumstantial activity and see the person of Jesus.

The raising of the dead.

The command he had recently uttered, 'take up your mat and walk,' would one day be eclipsed by a greater command to the dead to rise. And as the weakened muscles and sinews in that man's legs could not withstand the authority of the Creators words, neither will the dead be able to lie in their graves any longer. We know from other scriptures that this command to rise is the dawning of the age to come. Our times, past, present and future are in his hands.

The chapter close with the testimony of witnesses to the above claims.

Jesus himself. 5:31-32. Jesus spoke of himself but he conceded that it could be said that a madman would testify to himself. So, he leaves that aside.

John the Baptizer. 5:33-35. There was a day when they regarded him as a prophet of God, and he had testified as to who Jesus was, *'the one coming after me, who was before me.'*

The Miracles. 5:36-38. His argument was, if the works that I do for the benefit of mankind are not works of God, then whose works are they?

The Scriptures. 5:38-46. You search the scriptures but you do not find me. Jesus was saying that the scriptures identify the works that he was doing as works of God. Then he reasoned, if I am doing works already identified as works of God, why are they not works of God when I do them? The scriptures will be their judge because Moses wrote about Jesus. Deuteronomy 18:14-18.

4. The Feeding of the Five Thousand. 6:1-15;25-29

We usually call this Miraculous Sign the feeding of the five thousand. It is closely linked to the discourse that follows on the Bread of Life, which will discuss later.

In the first three signs an individual or very small group was benefitted; the manager of the feast, the nobleman's son, and the lame man at the pool. But here the beneficiaries of the sign are a vast crowd of over 5000 people.

It shows Jesus as Lord when the need is great.
We so often emphasise the truth that Jesus is interested in the small and few, we can overlook that he is also Lord when the need is great and involves many. So significant is this sign it is recorded in all 4 gospels. He is not only able to deal with the small things but could take on the big things as well. There is a precedent to this story in 2 Kings 4:42-45.

Another difference with this sign is that Jesus tries to involve his disciples in the working of the miracle rather than just doing it himself. This was a dramatic development in his ministry as he was preparing his disciples to continue the work when he would no longer be around.

He was saying; the crowds are here because I can perform miracles. He laments this fact in 6:26. They are here to see what I can do for them. But to his disciples he was saying 'how much have you believed about who I am.' As true as this is, this is not principally a story about the disciples, the crowd, or the boy and his lunch. It is a story that reveals something more about Jesus.

It was near the season of Passover, that is, late March, springtime.

'When Jesus looked up and saw a great crowd coming toward him, he said to Philip, *'Where shall we buy bread for these people to eat?" He asked this only to test him, for he already had in mind what he was going to do.'* Jesus was sort of saying, 'Philip from what you believe about me, what you have come to understand about me, if you were me, what would you do?'

If Philip had lived today the scene may have been something like this; Philip got out his calculator. 5000 people, rolls, white and brown, margarine; large tub, tomatoes; a lot, cheese; edam. At least two supermarket trucks full. And because

34

supermarkets had not yet been invented, he said, 'let us send them home!'

Actually, what he said was, "It would take more than half a year's wages to buy enough bread for each one to have a bite!" But it amounted to the same thing. The problem is too big for me to contemplate a solution. Another of his disciples, Andrew, Simon Peter's brother, spoke up, '*Here is a boy with five small barley loaves and two small fish, but how far will they go among so many?*' He was trying to be helpful. The sum of it was that Philip's faith scale was still zero, Andrew was a bit better. It seems that on the basis of the glimmer of faith that Andrew expressed, Jesus responded to the situation.

All our problems will always be unsurmountable until through believing we grasp how great the Son of God is. Jesus had the people sit down. He was going to show them once more who he was by what he did. He took the five sandwiches and fed the five thousand people. In fact, he made so many fish sandwiches they were fed up of fish sandwiches and there were 12 baskets left over.

Jesus was demonstrating that if he could feed five thousand, he could feed five million, or even everyone on earth. There was no limit to his capability. It was a prophetic glimpse into the age to come, '*where never again would they hunger, never again would they thirst.*' The power of the gospel was not going to run out like a cheap AA battery after the first few converts. His Grace would always be as powerful as it was for the first believers, to all believers.

Two thousand years later the gospel is the same today as it ever was. His power to heal, deliver, transform, and restore is as potent for us today who dare to believe, as it was for those who first believed.

He can take the little and make it plenty.

He can take the insignificant and make it important.

He can take the despised and make it vital.

He could have done it all by himself but he has chosen to involve his people in the outworking of his kingdom.

The vital thing in this incident was that Jesus wanted them to put something in his hand so he could display his Lordship when the need is greater than the supply.

There is a fascinating sequel to this story in Mark 8:14-21. This incident took place after this miracle and a subsequent miracle where four thousand were fed from seven loaves. It appears a little cryptic until we look at the evidence the account gives us.

- They had forgotten to bring bread.
- There was one loaf of bread in the boat.
- We have no bread.
- Jesus said to watch out for the yeast of the Pharisees and of Herod.
- They thought Jesus was upset because they had forgot to bring bread.

'Do you not see or understand.?' Jesus was testing their faith again to see how much they had believed about who he was and what he was capable of doing.

The loaf in the boat was important. It was obviously inedible because they knew it was there but spoke as if it wasn't. It had no value.

What Jesus was asking is this, 'what do you think I would have done if you had given the mouldy old loaf to me?'

Jesus asked them to remember what he did with the five loaves and the seven loaves, so what do you think I could have done with that mouldy loaf. Can you image that loaf in his hands, the mould disappears the dampness dries out and the loaf becomes all fluffy and fresh again, and that smell of freshly baked bread would have filled the boat, they could have had a loaf each or more, and they would all have had their lunch.

The Pharisees. Now they believed the bible as it was then, the Old Testament, was the word of God. The problem was they believed a whole lot of other stuff was God's word as well, traditions and the writings of the Rabbi's. Their whole faith was a matter of keeping rules.

The Herodians. Now their idea of religion was not to take it seriously, it was culture, it was custom, but it was not to be lived by. This was unbelief in the eyes of Jesus and prohibited the power of God working.

Now he added another dimension of unbelief, not putting things in God's hands. Thinking that it is not worth it, or he is not interested, or there is nothing he could do anyway.

Maybe we consider our needs, our crisis, our situation as not being important there is nothing that He could do to help us anyway. It's unbelief, and so we have a miracle that never happened.

Luke 8:49. When Jairus' daughter died they said, 'Don't bother the teacher anymore.' He could have healed her but she is now dead there is nothing he can do.

Mark 10:13-16. When the people brought their children to the disciples, they tried to turn them away, they were not worthy of the master's time. But Jesus rebuked them and said, 'let the children come unto me for the Kingdom of heaven belongs to them as well as to adults.'

Mark 10: 48. When blind Bartimaeus cried out they said, 'be quiet.'

I am not sure where Divine Sovereignty ends and human responsibility begins; that is, the things that God would do anyway without anyone's help, and things where he requires our participation. And because we do not know this boundary Jesus is teaching us to bring everything to him and let him sort it, just put it in his hands. Our valuation, estimation or priority is of no consideration.

The people wanted to make him king. It was the Red Cross, Red Crescent, United nations, Oxfam and World Vision all rolled into one. But Jesus went away. He berates them for wanting the produce of the miracle but not to believe in him as the Messiah. When asked, 'What must we do to work the works of God?' He replies, 'The work of God is to believe in the one whom he has sent.' Belief is not primarily thinking of what Jesus can do for me, but believing who he is and resting in the greatness and immensity of his grace. The needs of mankind are not too big for Jesus. Our complications will not outstretch his ability to solve. Jesus is Lord when the need outstrips the supply.

5. The Storm on the Lake. 6:16-24

This story leads us quickly into the 5th of the Miraculous Signs that reveal to us who Jesus is. In fact, this is a sort of interruption in the matter of the 'Bread of Life' discourse which follows next.

The walking on the water. The other gospels give us a much more detailed account of this phenomenal event. Matthew 14: 23-34; Mark 6: 45-56. Matthew adds the story of Peter walking on the water.

They both place the story in the same time scale, immediately after the feeding of the five thousand, and they both indicate that Jesus was trying to get away from the crowds for a time of solitude and prayer.

It shows Jesus as Lord over the Natural Order.

We are taken back to the words in the prologue, '*All things were made by him, there was not anything made he did not make.*'

They had delayed their journey until nightfall. Not the wisest time to set out on the lake when you had a significant number of people on board. The Lake is about 8 miles wide at its widest point and some 13 miles from north to south. It is subject to sudden weather changes. They were caught in a rising storm. It wasn't yet fatal, but it was about to be. It is difficult to identify the route they were taking as the place names differ in the Gospels and some of the places have not been located with certainty. Whatever, they had not gone far in their journey when they became exhausted against the prevailing weather.

Jesus displays his Lordship over the natural order by;

- walking on water, overriding gravity;
- walking against the wind faster than they could row, overriding the elements,
- by shortening the elapse of time so that instead of being in the middle of the lake they saw the harbour wall of Capernaum.

An interesting comment is found in Mark 6:52. *'They had not understood the loaves, their hearts were hardened.'* Jesus expected them to extrapolate the one miracle to apply to other situations. In other words, he was expecting them to understand that if he could feed the five thousand, then he could also see them safely through the storm. They had clearly not made this connection.

It was truly a spectacular miracle to see the elements which regulated their lives, be subject to the authority of the Son of God. Then the humanity of the Son of Man as he sat down in the boat to complete the journey.

Every possible situation that we can face is not depicted in the scriptures. There are many situations we find ourselves in today, that could not have been contemplated in biblical times. We are expected to employ the faith we have gained in one situation to whatever situation we find ourselves. These miraculous signs give us a panorama of who Jesus is so that we may believe in him, not just for these specific situations, but for all possible situations.

Whether it be an emotional storm, a mental storm, a spiritual storm or a physical storm that a person is passing through,

Jesus is not bound or limited by the forces unleashed in the storm. Many times, I have been exhausted in the storm. I just could not fight the wind of a situation any more. Then suddenly, Jesus came, and it was over, I had arrived at a safe place.

The disciples set out on a journey they really should not have set out considering the prevailing weather conditions. They embarked on the journey, it would seem from the other Gospels, at the request of Jesus. Maybe they thought that if Jesus told them to undertake the journey all would be well. He would never send them into danger. But as things evolved that was not the case. The truth that is revealed here is that even at the Masters bidding we can enter into danger. The promise is that he will come to us in the crisis and bring us to a safe place. The teaching is that he will complete the work that he has begun and we can forever hold on to the principles of this story as a basis of faith. If he wants you to go to 'Capernaum,' you will get to 'Capernaum' whatever storms come along the way.

6. The man born blind. 9:1-41

This is the sixth of the Miraculous Signs that Jesus performed so that his disciples may believe. John recorded them so that we may have the ability to believe in the same way. 20: 30-31.

This is a spectacular sign and a half, and what a disturbance it caused.

'*As he went along, he saw a man blind from birth. His disciples asked him, "Rabbi, who sinned, this man or his parents, that he was born blind?'*

This sign is to reveal Jesus as Lord over human misfortune.

The detail, 'blind from birth' is essential in understanding this story. This was the only recorded miracle of Jesus which involved the healing of a congenital condition.

What a question, 'Who sinned?' It exposes the common belief of then and now. Someone did something bad for someone to be born blind. Or more personally, 'what did I do to deserve this?' It also leads to the opposite conclusion that if I don't have any physical defects then I must be okay, I have not sinned.

They were asking, were the sins of the parents paid for by the misfortune of the child? They did have Exodus 20:4 as a basis for this part of the question. But Ezekiel 18 promises, in the Messianic age, this would not be the case. The other part of the question is more complex and reflects the possibility of some form of re-incarnation or the ability of the child to 'sin' in the womb. Some Jews sects believe in re-incarnation.[13]

Whatever, they add up to the fact that in their thinking, someone was to blame.

Neither. Jesus' answer is so important. This was not a result of anyone's individual sin, but a result of the depravity of human nature as it had been separated from God by the disobedience of Adam. As we would understand today, the genetic code sometimes gets it wrong and produces life that is contradictory to what we would generally call 'normal.' The genetic process is merciless, it produces what it does and it is up to the person concerned to make the best of it.

We shall see shortly that the belief in blame was fundamental to the way the man was subsequently treated. His condition, it was believed, placed him in a certain stratum of society and it should never be interfered with.

This happened. Firstly; what happened? The man was born blind so that when Jesus came along, he could display the

---

[13] **Chabad.org**

work of God? That is so bizarre, to think God would engineer a lifetime of blindness just so Jesus could heal him.

'What happened?' Jesus and his disciples came in contact with the man. At that moment in time, they happened to be in the same street, at the same time, that's what happened. Jesus said this is an opportunity to display the work of God by facing a matter beyond anyone's control. In other words, this was not accidental or coincidental, but God arranged the encounter, that Jesus with healing power met the man who was blind from birth. This was a moment of divine appointment wherein Jesus took the opportunity to show us more of himself. We can learn from this that all the things that have happened to us, over which we had no control may be laid at the feet of the Master Healer.

Secondly, he made some mud with saliva and the dust of the ground. Now the saliva or dust did not heal him. This is revealing who Jesus is. It is a picture of God making the first man from the dust of the ground, a perfect man, and amongst other things an Adam that could see. Symbolically he takes this man back to the beginning by-passing the generations of genetic distortion that caused his blindness and creates his eyes anew. Jesus is revealed as the creator once more, 'all things were made by him.'

Thirdly he sends him to the Pool of Siloam. (note not Bethesda) The word Siloam means 'Sent'. It was revealing Jesus as the one 'Sent.' Jesus was 'the Siloam.' Jesus was sent from the Father, from the beginning, and was sent to be the Saviour of the world. Jesus was restoring the weakness of the first creation with a new creation and 'sent' the man into a new future where he would be able to see.

He washed and came back seeing. The healing was not in the waters of Siloam either. The healing was in the words of Jesus. It was like the other miracles pointing to the age to come and the Kingdom of the Messiah. '*Then shall the eyes of the blind be opened.*' Why did Jesus send him to the pool?

So that the family, the neighbours and the Jewish leaders could see the miracle.

What a fuss this created. The Jewish leaders were apoplectic with rage. They questioned the man; they questioned the neighbours. They were reluctant to confirm that he was the man they saw every day. They said he looked like the blind man. They questioned the parents. They also would not make a categoric statement. But at least they owned that this was their son and he once was blind. They asked the man himself. In fact, they asked him over and over. They got so upset with him because he would not deny that it was Jesus that had healed him. He finally utters that definitive statement, *'One thing I know, I once was blind but now I see.'* We have the unusual situation of an ordinary man taking on the Jewish leaders and pointing out rather convincingly, the stupidity of their argument. Everyone else involved was afraid to speak out the obvious truth. The man's conclusion was that only God could open blind eyes therefore Jesus was sent from God.

Why were the Leaders so incensed at the healing of this man? Firstly, it was on the Sabbath. We have already learned that keeping the Sabbath was more important to these people than helping their fellowman, and why Jesus seemed to perform miracles on the Sabbath. But on this occasion, this was not the main reason for their protest.
Secondly, *'We don't know where he came from.'* We shall see that this objection arises again later as the main issue in another debate. But for now, suffice it to say, they knew Jesus wasn't one of them, therefore he could not have God's approval. He was an imposter in the religion of which they were sole custodians. 9:28-29.
But the main cause of their response was that it upset their idea of the order of things.

As we have seen they were obsessed with the idea of cause and effect. This man was blind as a punishment. 9:34. The Jewish leaders were not blind; no punishment had befallen them. So, they were righteous.

The problem lay in the fact that this man was designated a sinner because he was blind. He was now no longer blind, so what happens to his status as a sinner? Jesus had removed the punishment so who was going to pay for the sin that had supposedly been committed. This man was now equal with them in that he had no physical disability, yet, in their estimation, he had sinned. The effect of sin was removed. The sentence of sin was cancelled. A man walked free and no price was paid. This they could not grasp, because they didn't know who Jesus was.

We can now begin to see that this miracle and its implications had dismantled the entire structure or what Judaism had become under the Pharisees. Everything they believed about sin and righteousness was blasted to pieces. They could not let this situation continue so they excommunicated the man from the religion of Israel.

9:39-41. 'The blind will see, and those who see will become blind.' In the context of this story the Pharisees had equated sin with blindness and sight with righteousness.

Jesus was proclaiming the core message of the Gospel that through him and his forthcoming atoning death, sinners will be made righteous, as if they had never sinned. Yet hose who believed they were righteous because of their adherence to a law, were in fact judged as sinners.

This is such a powerful revelation of who Jesus is. The misfortunes of life do not condemn us as sinners. Whatever has happened to a person has no bearing on their right to become a child of God and know the forgiveness of sins. The gospel is for all except those who judge themselves righteous without it. Their guilt remains.

Jesus finds the man and brings the whole incident to its ultimate conclusion, 'Do you believe.' 9:35-38. He believed and worshipped him.

When you believe who Jesus is, God made flesh; the creator saviour; the mouthpiece of God; and the atoning sacrifice for the sin of the world, then the idea of him cancelling the effect of Adam's sin as if it never happened, removing the disability that sin caused, and causing him to walk as a new creation becomes a real and present possibility

7. The raising of Lazarus. 11: 1-44

This is seventh and last of the Miraculous Signs that John selected to tell us about so that we may believe as he had believed. The healing miracles had become more and more profound from a man who had been afflicted for a long time, to someone afflicted from birth, and finally someone who had already succumbed to death.

This is arguably the greatest of all the signs, and shows Jesus as the Lord over Death. Jesus has shown himself to be Lord over the phenomena of the natural world, now he shows himself as Lord in the spiritual realms as well.

The account begins with a message from Bethany, that Lazarus, Mary and Martha's brother, was seriously ill. Jesus was very close to this family, yet he did not leave immediately to go to them. Instead, he said, *'this sickness will not end in death. No, it is for God's glory, so that God's Son may be glorified through it. '*

Jesus was in no rush. He saw the bigger picture. It seems that Jesus knew already that Lazarus was dead. We are faced with the truth that there was something greater than the well-being of the sisters and the health of Lazarus and that was the Glory, or the Renown of God. Jesus waited until his death would be beyond question and a crowd of people would have gathered.

In returning to the prologue, the words '*In him was life, and his life was the light of men*' jump out at us. His life was more than a functioning biology. His life was the life of the Living God. It could function here on earth and it could function in the heavenly realms as well. He showed death to be a separation from life on earth but not a cessation of being. As much as he was Lord over life in this world, he was Lord over life in the next as well.

Lazarus was identified by reference to his sister Mary. Clearly John assumed that his readers would know full well who Mary was and the significant thing she did because her action was to be told wherever the Gospel was preached. Matthew 26:13. Martha and Lazarus were less well known and needed introduction. There was clearly a close relationship between Jesus and this sibling family. Much more had obviously taken place than is recorded in the Gospels to cause this relationship to come about. This is the first time that the miracles of Jesus concerned someone he knew well, with possible exception of the wedding at Cana. The sisters believed. Martha was convinced God would give Jesus anything he asked for.

Mary believed that Lazarus would not have died if Jesus had been there. But neither she or Martha could comprehend the raising of the dead. If Jesus had come when Lazarus was ill, they believed that was within the scope of Jesus power to restore him. If Jesus had come when Lazarus was close to death, they believed that was also within his known ability to heal. But Jesus wanted to demonstrate that even though Lazarus had passed from this life to the next, he still had the power to intervene.

In showing his power over death it would help to prepare them to face his death and resurrection, the matter of their own death and resurrection, and ultimately the matter of the final resurrection at the end of the age.

Another factor is brought to our attention in that he had left Judea earlier for safety reasons and he was now compelled to return, this seemed to Thomas a least, a fateful decision. He had good reason to be concerned.

God's Delay.

Why did Jesus take so long to return to Bethany? God's delays are a mystery to us but we know it is a fact of life. A really descriptive account of an apparent Divine Delay is found in Daniel 10: 1-14. Here we see the angel of the Lord was delayed by 21 days. The reason we understand to be a spiritual battle in the heavenly realms with the powers of evil. Maybe this confrontation with death at Bethany was not as simple as the story relates. Maybe Jesus needed spiritual preparation for the encounter that was about to take place, knowing it would lead inextricably to his own death. Whatever the reason, Jesus assures the disciples that death would not have the last word.

'Your brother will rise again.' To which Martha replies with her faith in the final resurrection. Jesus replied and said, 'I am that resurrection,' a statement we shall examine later.

Many believers constantly pray for revival, but never seem to be able to step into revival. Many believe there will be dark and troublesome days before Jesus returns, but never think we may already be in those fateful days. All believers speak of going to heaven when they die, but many also do everything they can to delay the inevitability. What I am saying, like Martha, we keep momentous moments in the future because we can't quite believe that they can come now. Jesus said that he was going to bring that great and momentous day of the resurrection, in part, to Bethany that day.

Jesus walked the mourner's road and wept with them. Jesus' tears were not tears of loss and desperation as theirs were, his tears were tears for their tears. He wept because sin and death had reduced humanity to despair in the face of death.

He prayed a prayer for the benefit of the people. What was about to happen was not a miracle in isolation, but a miracle worked in conjunction with the God they worshipped. *'Father you have heard me, I knew that you always hear me, but I said this for the benefit of the people standing here, that they may believe you sent me.'* 11:41-42. He was with God, he was God, he became flesh. So, he called Lazarus from the tomb. Lazarus was restored to the position in life he had before. He was not immortal; he would die again. Mary, Martha, and Lazarus rejoiced in what had happened, but they would have to walk this road again. The overriding purpose of the miracle was to show the Glory of God through Jesus as Lord over death.

Death is not final. It is the transition from this life to the next. There is nothing to fear because the Lord of this life is the Lord of the next. Death is more like sleeping as far as Jesus is concerned, there will be an awakening. The raising of the dead was more of a witness to the glory of God than the healing of the sick. What he did to Lazarus was a type of what will happen to all believers on the last day.

The result of this demonstration of the Glory of God. A new objection to Jesus was now vocalised. The Jewish leaders planned to put both Jesus and Lazarus to death because they feared the whole nation would go after them and the Romans would come and wipe them out as a people. It was thought it to be better to live a compromised existence under the dominance of Rome, than to enter into the reality of the Kingdom which Jesus preached, and fear the wrath of Rome. What they were particularly worried about of course, was not the people and their relationship with God but their own lucrative positions which be taken away from them and given to Jesus and his disciples.

A similar choice faces Christianity today. A fearsome force has arisen which demands we do not speak of the pertinent matters of righteousness and judgement as they may offend. The temptation is to keep quiet, but still exist, rather than stand up and face the inevitable persecution but declare the truth.

Caiaphas' speech.

'It is better for one that man to die for the people and that the whole nation perish.' This is an incredible statement and I doubt that even Caiaphas understood what he had said. What he meant was, let's put Jesus to death and that will solve the matter of people following him and antagonising Rome. Then we can all carry on as before.

What he actually said was a prophetic statement about what the death of Jesus would accomplish as substitutionary atonement for the sins of Israel and the entire world.

That can be why, in this age, such manifestations of the glory of God before an unbelieving public happen, but there are relatively rare. When people who think they hold the power of life and death find out there is a Power greater than themselves, they turn to genocide. They set in motion a plan to put Jesus to death. Jesus slows down the process by moving to a remote place before he sets foot on the inevitable journey to the cross.

This is the ultimate revelation of who Jesus is. World powers at that time or the time in which we live will not have the final say about the destiny of humanity. Whoever may feel that they have the power to steer what we do or do not do, believe or do not believe, will find out that they will be destroyed by the brightness of his coming, and the kingdoms of this world will become the kingdoms of our Lord Jesus Christ and he will reign.

This is the Jesus whom we serve, love and worship. We have truly seen his glory in these seven great Signs.

He is Lord over human shortcomings, when human effort runs out and the work is not complete. He is Lord over distance between the need and the supply. He is Lord over the ravages time can impart. He is Lord over human misfortune when we suffer for things beyond our control. He is Lord when the need is great and the resources are small. He is Lord over the natural world, suspending the laws of nature if they impede his Divine purpose. He is Lord in this life and the next, in this world and the world to come.

CHAPTER 4.
SEVEN PERSONAL
ENCOUNTERS

We now consider the second category of events that John selected for us to read so that we might believe. There is no miracle in any of these interviews, just a conversation that paints a word picture of some aspect of Jesus, that impacted John and brought him to belief.

1. The encounter with Nicodemus. 2:24-3:21.

It is important we do not lose sight of the reason John selected these encounters. The story is not primarily about Nicodemus but about Jesus. **We can see that the theme of the conversation is Heavenly things and Earthly things.**
It begins with the understanding Jesus knew what was in the hearts of people. He had encountered a group of people that appreciated his miraculous signs but made no steps to believe in him as the Son of God. Now he encounters Nicodemus and immediately recognises a sincere heart. Jesus will be available to the one who approaches him in sincerity of heart, he came to dispense the right to become a child of God to all those who would believe, and withhold it from those who would not. Nicodemus comes with that vitally important approach, to honour Jesus for who he was, not only for what he did. Nicodemus has already concluded that Jesus has been 'with God' as he addresses him as a man sent from God.

This encounter did not take place right at the beginning of Jesus' ministry as its setting in John suggests. Sufficient ministry and miracles had taken place for Nicodemus to give them careful consideration, come to certain conclusions and formulate certain questions.

Nicodemus approached Jesus by saying, '*We know.*' We may ask, who are 'we'? The answer must have been, that there were a group of people from among the Jewish leaders who had considered the ministry of Jesus and concluded that it was a visitation of God. This immediately elevates Nicodemus from an isolated individual to a representative of a like-minded group. 12:42.

Jesus also introduces the plural into the conversation in his response 3:10-11. '*We speak of what we know and we testify to what we have seen.*' We can ask again, 'Who are 'we'?' John said, Jesus was with God and Jesus was God, the same was in the beginning with God'

Can the 'we' mean the Father and the Holy Spirit? He had come to say what God wanted said and he had seen what God had seen. Certainly, as we are discovering, one of the great bones of contention the Jewish leaders had with Jesus was, by what authority did he speak and where did he come from in order to say such things.

What an encounter, the ambassador of the combined wisdom of some of the Jewish leadership, and the Ambassador of Almighty God, face to face, one dark night in old Jerusalem.

The way Jesus responds seems very curt. But we must understand it in the light of 2:24, '*he knew all men.*' He knew Nicodemus' heart and he knew the dilemma about which he had come to speak was between the Kingdom the Jewish leaders envisioned and the Kingdom of which he spoke. One was an earthly thing, the other a heavenly thing. To see the Kingdom of which Jesus spoke, manifest itself, you needed to be born anew.

Nicodemus got it. The Kingdom of which Jesus spoke needed a spiritual encounter which would enable a man to start life over anew with his past forgiven and the guilt and shame taken away.

He wasn't suggesting a physical re-birth, that was absurd. What he was saying was, as the absurd is not possible, I am a man of mature years, is it not too late for me to have such an encounter? Can I leave my prejudices, beliefs, obligations, responsibilities and traditions to start anew?

Jesus was saying that there was no other way into his Kingdom except through a new birth. This new birth was by definition, to be born of water and the Spirit.

The water was the water of baptism.

Specifically, the baptism of John the Baptizer. This was a problem for Nicodemus. Luke 7:30. The Pharisees had rejected the need for John's baptism.

Jesus didn't say this but the following is clearly implied;

'You have come to me by night, secretly, hoping matters can be sorted out under the cover of darkness. But I tell you it must be public in the 'Light' for all to see. Your declaration of repentance from self-righteousness, your symbolically going down into water, a realm of death, and arising anew in resurrection, the old gone and a heart set on knowing God anew, must be seen publicly. That is where it must begin.'

Then the next stage is also spoken of by the Baptist.

An encounter with the Holy Spirit.

An encounter that changes the heart of man from the inside. The law tries to change a man from the outside, but all it does is control the actions by discipline. The work of the Holy Spirit causes a man to desire righteousness, mercy, compassion, truth, and holiness from the deepest chambers of the heart. It makes him unafraid of repentance, restitution, and confession and what others think of it. It causes him to recoil from public displays of piety for applause and to just do what is on God's heart without recourse to praise.

Flesh gives birth to flesh. Humanly speaking one generation produces the next, but they are all born under the dislocation from God caused by Adam's disobedience

The Spirit gives birth to spirit. Each person comes into God's Kingdom not by generational birth, but by each having an encounter with God by the Holy Spirit. Each believer is a first-generation believer, because each is personally filled with the Holy Spirit. The wind blows where it will. You cannot source it, because it comes from heaven. Neither can you mark its destiny because it returns to heaven. So is the man born of the Spirit, he is caught up in heavenly things.

Nicodemus' jaw must have hit the ground by now because Jesus said, *'don't be surprised.'* This is what we know. You believe it and enter the Kingdom; you reject it and you will never enter the Kingdom. I have told you heavenly things with earthly examples and you have not believed, how will you believe in I only speak of heavenly things.

Jesus then gives another picture of heavenly things. The Son of man came down from heaven. The Son of man is sole authority on what heaven desires. The Son of Man is both man and God.

Moses and the snake. 3:15

Just as Moses lifted up the snake in the wilderness, (that is an earthly thing) so the Son of Man must be lifted up so that everyone who believes may have eternal life in him. (that is, a heavenly thing)

This refers to a miracle in the Old Testament. Numbers 21:4-9. In order to stop a plague of snakes God told Moses to impale the image of a snake on a high pole. Whoever looked up to the image on the pole and maintained their gaze on its meaning would be healed of the plague.

In the same way the Son of Man must be lifted up. The lifting up of the serpent image was to indicate to the people, the dilemma, and the answer to their dilemma, had come from heaven. The lifting up of the Son of Man was to indicate the same thing, the answer to the sin of man was a gift from God. They key phrase, I believe, is intended to be 'look up.'

The snake image was not only lifted up it was impaled to the stake.

It does not escape us to see that the image on the pole bore the likeness of the creatures that had caused the problem. When Jesus hung on the cross, he looked no different to the people who put him there, the thieves on either side of him, or to the people that passed by. He had taken on the same form. He was theirs and our, representative.

It cannot be expressed any more succinctly than in the words of Isaiah 53

> *He had no beauty or majesty to attract us to him, nothing in his appearance that we should desire him. He was despised and rejected by mankind, a man of suffering, and familiar with pain.*
> *Like one from whom people hide their faces he was despised, and we held him in low esteem.*
> *Surely, he took up our pain and bore our suffering, yet we considered him punished by God, stricken by him, and afflicted. But he was pierced for our transgressions.*

Now let's put this together. Jesus the Son of God, the Word from the beginning, the Light of the World, full of grace and Truth, the overcomer of darkness, the only one to come from heaven to earth, is to be seen as one impaled upon a stake, bearing the likeness of sinners.

In this way, the Son of Man must be lifted up. The lifting up of the Son of Man has several applications. 12:30-34. It meant both the cross and the ascension. Clearly the 'lifting up' spoke of triumph, authority, prestige and prominence. But in the simplicity of the comparison to the snake of Moses, it simply meant; 'he had come from above.' As John had just recorded, 'the one who came down from heaven.

Jesus shared with the sincere heart of Nicodemus these 'heavenly things' no one else had ever seen before. Belief in Jesus was more than acknowledging he was a man sent from God. He was God and he was man. It was more than seeing him as a great prophet or worker of miracles. The belief that would take hold of a person's life and transform it so that it was like he had been born all over again, was to grasp that the Son of God had come to be an atoning sacrifice for the sin of all who would believe, so that they could be free to enter the kingdom of God and enjoy the gift of heavenly things which would secure an everlasting relationship with God.

Nicodemus abruptly disappears at this point, not to return to the scene until he offers a tentative defence of Jesus in 7:50 and then in the 'lifting up of Jesus' at the crucifixion. Nicodemus along with Joseph of Arimathea took responsibility for the burial of Jesus' body. 19:39. This account tells us that Jesus is the one who reveals of heavenly things.

3:16-21. We have become so accustomed to quoting John 3:16 as a 'stand-alone' verse we forget that it is inextricably linked to verse 15 on the one side and verse 17 on the other. **For God so loved.** I would contend the 'so' is not an emphatic word, in that, God loved the world so much; as the Good News and Living Bible put it. But rather it is comparative, as in Nestles Greek text, 'For thus loved God the world; and in Holman and NLT, 'God loved the world in this way.' In this sense it maintains the flow from verse 15. We should bear this in mind when we return to the common English rendering, *'For God so loved world.'*

We now find several references to the words of the prologue summing up this conversation.

'The World.' Let us step slowly and carefully through the implications of this word. 'The Cosmos.' John uses the word 'world' more than any other NT writer. It plainly does not have a single meaning.

1:10. *'He was in the world.'* Meaning he lived on planet earth.
4:42. *'Saviour of the world.'* Meaning he was the Saviour of all people.
12:19. *'Whole world.'* Meaning the Nation of Israel, but obviously a hyperbole.
12:30 *'the prince of this world.'* Meaning a force that influenced the minds of many people.
There are other uses but what does it mean here in 3:16?
What was this 'world' that God loved? Was it the planet; the Jews; the Jews and Gentiles; a specific community among the people of the world, such as those who would believe; or every single man or woman ever born or whoever would be born?
1:10 *tells us, 'He was in the world and though the world was made through him, the world did not recognise him'* What world did he make? He did not create the world as it had become, and as he found it, one that could not recognise the creator.
As the snake was a symbol of Jesus, the plague infested people were a picture of the sinful state of humanity. The ancient people had rebelled against God and as a result God sent the snakes. Only those who had been bitten, repented and then looked up at the snake on the pole were healed. The method of deliverance was also sent by God to benefit those who repented. Not everyone survived.

This, then, is how God loves the world.
God did not love the world as it had become, neither did he love the forces of evil or the people that had made it so. In fact, John tells us in 3:36, God's wrath remains on them unless they repent. The default state of humanity is to abide

under the wrath of God. Romans 1:18-32; 2:8; Ephesians 2:1-3. God's love was for people throughout the earth (whosoever) who had both contributed to the worlds state and were at the same time victims of it, but were prepared to repent and believe in the One whom God had sent to be the Saviour. To those, and those only, he would grant the gift of Eternal Life. The world that God loved was the world as it had been designed and would one day be again. The people God loved were those who would believe in him and by their dedication to him, help to being that world about.

This is the magnitude of God's love. He faced the people on the earth in righteous anger because of the perpetration and promulgation of sin, but he chose to stay his anger for a time with love, so that all who will could participate of his Grace. This 'love' of God was not an uncontrollable passion but a decision to love in spite of sin.

Every miracle that Jesus performed lifted a person or persons from the world as it had become and as it had affected them, into the world as it was designed to be. It all pointed to a day, yet to come, when there will be a new heaven and a new earth and the former things will have passed away. This is the essence of the Kingdom of God. It is the world to come, but the power of the Gospel of Jesus Christ has enabled glimpses and moments of that world to impact us now, which are identified by our experiences through the Holy Spirit. On that day there will be no sin; today we can overcome sin. On that day there will be health; today we can know healing. On that day Satan will be bound forever; today we can defeat him in Jesus' name.

To be born again, or born anew, or born from above, whichever phrase means the most to you, is essential, to escape the consequences of the wrath of God.

Jesus is the only one to come from the Father and the only one to return to the Father's side. As he was later to say, '**no one comes to the Father but by me.**'

He who believes.
Belief in the lifting up of the Son of Man is the fact of the matter. Belief is the crucial thing. Belief in who he is, where he came from, what he did, and where he is going, gains eternal life. 'Eternal,' is not particularly expressing that which will last forever, but by default of course it does, the point of emphasis is a quality of life that belongs to the Eternal One.

Not perish.
To perish is to wither as a branch cut from its life source. Slowly the life ebbs away until nothing of value remains, except to be burnt. Unbelief will bring about a situation wherein all contact and relationship with God will cease. The unbeliever is unaware of just how much he is a beneficiary of the Grace of God while he lives. It will be when life is over and he remains in unbelief, he will truly understand what it is to be cut off from God.

Not to condemn.
Jesus did not come to pronounce condemnation; he came to announce the gift of eternal life. While the Hand of God's wrath is stayed, the Grace that is given for Salvation also affects those who refuse to believe, it does not save them while they are in unbelief, but it shelters them from the effect of his wrath. We see that those who refuse to believe are already condemned by that action. They were condemned before Jesus came and they remain condemned after he came if they do not believe.

Lovers of darkness hate the light.
These comments are in reverse order describing a person's journey away from God. The first steps away from God are when we love the darkness, the darkness being the things that are opposed to the character of God. To embrace that lifestyle brings condemnation and condemnation cause one to perish.

The Light is the Life that has shone in the darkness. It is the life and character of Jesus. There are those who run towards it, unconcerned about what it exposes, because what is given is far greater than that which is taken away. And there are those who run from it, more concerned about what can be exposed than that which can be imparted.

We have this understanding of Jesus as the One who has brought to us, heavenly things, or things that have come down from heaven.

Baptism

The text returns us for a short while to the activity of John the Baptizer. We have the interesting scenario where Jesus and his disciples, and the Baptist and his disciples are baptizing in the same vicinity.

The matter is recorded here because it follows from the teaching to Nicodemus that a public baptism was required in order to step into the Kingdom of God. Maybe Nicodemus and his friends came to be baptised. Whatever the case the picture before us is that of transition from the prophets of old to the Messiah of the new. The lessening of the activity of the one and the increasing of the activity of the other. If there was ever a singular point at which the Old Testament gave way to the New, then this is surely it.

It tells us something about John. We can underestimate the influence of John the Baptiser. After all, in Acts 19:1-7. We have a reference to a 'church of believers' in Ephesus who were apparently followers of the Baptist. It is remarkable that such a group could exist for so long after John's death and so far from Israel.

He knew his place. Always remember our ministry will not go on forever. It is more likely to be seasonal than perennial. When a chapter comes to an end, lay down your responsibility with grace and pass on everything you have to those who will follow after you. Our attitude should be like John. It is not our fame and success that is important. It is that those who follow on, are equipped to carry the task until Jesus comes again.

It tells us something about Jesus.

This was not an aggressive takeover. This was not a 'move over I am here now.' It is important that when a person enters the role of any ministry, they are respectful of what went on before. Our predecessors did what God called them to do in their generation and time of influence, according to the revelation granted to them. We, likewise, must be careful to do what God has called us to do in the time allotted to us, not in competition to what has gone before, but in fulfilment. We can say that Jesus stood on the shoulders of John.

John largely brought truth and light to earthly things. Luke 3:7-13. Jesus brought truth and light to heavenly things. 3:31-35.

2. The Woman at the Well. 4:1-42.

The second encounter that John records for us is the interview with the Samaritan Woman. Remember it is recorded so that we may believe who Jesus is, and in believing have life in his name. Once again this is not a story about the woman but a revelation about Jesus. **It tells us that he knows everything about our situation.**

This reveals Jesus, a light in the darkness. John has told us that in him was life and his life was the light of men. This light has shone in the darkness, and the darkness has not been able to absorb it. He shone light on a well which changed the way we see God. He shone a light on a woman that drove out the darkness that gripped her. He shone light on a political hostility that showed something glorious to come. He shone a light on what energised him revealing the ultimate purpose of why he had come from heaven.

He needed to go through Samaria. That is not a geographical thing. There were other ways to Galilee that would avoid Samaria. It was a spiritual thing. He was not simply going from Judea to Galilee through Samaria. He had come from heaven to Samaria to meet this woman. Light enables us to see things as they are. Spiritual light enables us to see things as God sees them. Jesus reveals his all-encompassing knowledge.

It was midday. As much as this was a divinely appointed mission Jesus still got tired and sat down to rest a while. A woman came to draw water. This person could not be in more contrast to Nicodemus. Principally, Nicodemus came to meet a man sent from God. This woman had no intention of meeting a man sent from God or anyone else for that matter, she came to a well to draw water. But Jesus was as much at home with the woman as he was with the Pharisee. This is remarkable from the perspective that Jews and Samaritans did not socialise. They despised each other. It was a historical thing passed on from generation to generation over hundreds of years. In the parable of Jesus, (Luke 10:25-37) we see that Jesus placed the 'good guy' as a Samaritan, and the 'bad guys' as the Jews. Jesus was not saying that the one was better than the other, but they both had fallen short of God's standards, they both needed to step into the kingdom of God, and both were invited to believe on the Saviour. This would, of course, have infuriated the Jews. We can see this when they tried to insult him by calling him 'a Samaritan and demon possessed.' 8:45.

But Jesus had not come from Jerusalem, or from Mount Gerizim, the shrine of the Samaritans, he had come down from heaven

The woman was well informed of the prejudice. As soon as Jesus spoke asking for a drink of water, she retreated to the status quo. 'Don't you know, the Jews and Samaritans have no dealings with each other. How can you ask me for a drink?' We have said that this passage reveals the fact that Jesus knows all about our situation. It is ironic that she hints that there is something he did not know. His knowledge is revealed at each step.

He knew the history better than she did.

'If you only knew the gift of God and who it is that asks you for a drink.'

Our world has many people groups who are bound by generational hatred. Two people who have done no harm to each other, remember what their fathers did, or their grandfathers or even further back, and they must 'balance the account.' And so, the hatred is birthed in another generation and people continue to die. This is a terrible state of affairs, which unfortunately, we are all too familiar. Jesus' approach is like this; 'our fathers did what they did and they will have to answer to God for it.' We also have the free choice to do what we do, we are not our fathers' prisoners, and we will have to give account to God for what we do.'

'If you knew what I know.' God had given this lady a gift, right there, at that moment, at that well. It's the same gift as he has given the Jews, a way of salvation not through the traditions of one's ancestors, but to meet him personally and directly oneself. We don't approach God as collective groups; we approach God as individuals. The solitariness of this woman illustrates this. She no longer had to live under the shadow of the group with which she identified. She could stand out in the Light of God's presence as a whole complete person whom God loved very much. One generation cannot believe, or not believe, for another. The result of the woman's witness emphasises this when the folk of the town confessed, *'we no longer believe because of what you said, now we have heard for ourselves.'*

Jesus of course is the gift of God. *'God so loved the world he gave.'* If this woman had known who Jesus was, she would have asked him for a drink.

He knew of a water that was not in the well.

You have nothing to draw with, how can you give me water. Are you greater than our Father Jacob? Now there is a leading question if there ever was one.

Jacob gave this woman's ancestors a gift. The well. It had served them faithfully ever since. That was a gift from God. It was also the place where Joseph had been interred when the nation returned from Egypt. Joshua 24 :32. Hence, it would seem that this place was also a sort of shrine to the ancestors of the past.

Jesus offered this woman the gift of eternal life. It would transform her and set her free from her history to serve God in her generation. This was a greater gift from God. Jesus describes it as 'living water.' This gift would not come out of the well, but down from heaven

'Everyone who drinks this water will be thirsty again, but whoever drinks the water I give them will never thirst. Indeed, the water I give them will become in them a spring of water welling up to eternal life.' 4:13. Once more we see Jesus speaking of heavenly things with earthly examples.

I think she got it. She got the analogy. Jesus was speaking of a spiritual experience that would satisfy her deepest longings, and most of all grant her a personal encounter with God. It seems possible that she was saying, give me your gift that I may find a life that is not tied to the drudgery of every day routine and memories of the past. In a moment she would put down the water jar and return to the town with a message of 'living water.'

He knew her personal history.

'Go call your husband.' I find it hard to believe this woman was a promiscuous a-moral, wanton woman as many commentators picture her. It seems to me she was a victim of her circumstances and the cruel way the society in which she lived dealt with it. Jesus was not unmasking her shame but releasing her pain. The end of five marriages could no way be her fault, she had no power to terminate a marriage.[14] She had not committed adultery otherwise she would likely have

---

[14] **Israel Institute for Biblical Studies**

been stoned to death. Her husbands must have died. She remarried because that was the custom. She had been left ultimately destitute. The pain haunted her, but some kindly soul had taken her in so she would not starve to death. The only thing that could be laid at her door was her present relationship. That is what she meant when she said, *'come see a man that told me everything I ever did.'* He knows what I have done and why. She doesn't seem to have been a despised reject of society, because she was able to persuade the people of her town to come to meet Jesus.

Jesus knows what has happened to you, the sins you have committed, the mistakes you have made; but more so, the things that happened to you beyond your control that have marked you, shaped you and made you into the person you have become. The pain, unfairness, the heritage passed on to you. The way the group you are identified with has defined you. He reveals them not to embarrass you, but to take them away and set you free to be the person God wants you to be. We are guilty of our own sin but often we are the victims of the sins of others. That is the effect of his 'living water, welling up to everlasting life.' It restores dignity and self-worth Surely, she said, 'this is the Messiah.'

Thirdly he knew of a worship that was neither Jewish or Samaritan.

The Samaritan bible consisted only of the books of Moses, and their customs were those found in those books. All they knew of the prophecies of the coming Messiah were what was recorded in Deuteronomy 18:17,18.

She knew nothing of the great prophecies of Isaiah, hence Jesus said, *'you worship what you do not know.'* When Jesus added, *'We worship what we do know.'* It wasn't a one upmanship statement. He was simply saying we have more of the scriptures, so we have access to more information. You have a hope of a Messiah but know nothing about him. You say this mountain, Mount Gerizim, the Jews say Jerusalem is the holy place. As for now the Jews have the better grasp of truth but both are about to be superseded by a kind of worship neither have dreamt about. Worship in Spirit and Truth. Men and women of all nations, cleansed from sin by the blood of Christ's atoning sacrifice; will approach God without ritual or sacrifices except that of a humble and contrite heart. God will not be a God of the place, but a God of the heart of the believer where he will dwell by the Holy Spirit. Such people filled with the Spirit of God will be the New Temple of worship. 1Corinthians 6:19.

Fourthly he knew of a food they knew nothing about.

We learn that Jesus stopped at this place because he was weary, speaking to us of his humanity. He was burdened with the same limitations as everyone else. The disciples had purchased food and tried to persuade him to eat. Once again, he uses an earthly example of a heavenly truth. 'My food is to do the will of him who sent me.'

The 'food' he spoke of was the fulfilment of his mission. The drawing of men to the Father by his message and ministry. Here is the thing they could not see, the message of the life-giving gospel was to be to all people, not just Jews. It was for those near the truth and those for from the truth. People who found themselves enemies would become one in Christ. The fields are ripe for harvest.

It is feasible that the references to the sower and the reaper are once again indicating John the Baptiser. Jesus acknowledges that John laid the foundation for the gospel of the Kingdom of God. In a spiritual sense John had broken the grip of spiritual darkness that covered the land so that Jesus could come and reap the harvest. Both John and Jesus would rejoice together over what was accomplished.

3. The Woman caught in Adultery. 8:1-11

The next encounter John selected is the account of the woman caught committing adultery. Most modern bibles point out that this account is not found in many of the earliest and otherwise most reliable manuscripts.[15] Many notable NT scholars therefore reject the authenticity of the text. However, the details, tone, and dialogue of the text of this story are entirely compatible with the Jesus we have come to know. There is nothing done or said that we would find contradictory to the way the Pharisees are represented elsewhere, or the way Jesus is portrayed elsewhere.

This is unlike the other omission of text we came across in the healing at Bethesda 5:4. Although we can accept that God may have well sent an Angel to disturb the water, what is not compatible with the God of the bible is that a competition was then set up in order for someone to be healed. Furthermore, such a 'competition' was designed to benefit the fittest and strongest. That is entirely contradictory to the God of the Bible we have come to know.   But this passage is entirely compatible with the Jesus we have come to know. So, whether John wrote it or not, no one knows definitely, but it is so intrinsically entwined in the ethos of the Gospel narrative I will treat this as an authentic account of John's revelation of who Jesus is.

It shows Jesus who is able to take away the guilt and power of sin.

We must note that John has chosen a second encounter with a woman, definitely guilty of sin, but, like the woman at the well, also a victim of the society that prevailed in the community in which she lived.

---

[15] **John the Gospel of Belief. Tenney.**

The scene is set. Jesus is teaching in the public area of the temple courts and is interrupted by the Pharisees, who made a woman stand before him and the crowd, and said, *'we caught her in the act of adultery, Moses said she should be stoned, what do you say?'*

Clearly this is not an attempt to obtain justice for the woman but to trap Jesus as John informs us. They knew enough about Jesus to know he would be inclined forgive her, but in so doing he would break Moses' Law. This is the trap they intended to spring.

Jesus rection is amazing. He seemed to ignore them and wrote with his finger in the dust of the ground. It does not escape our notice that the law in question was originally written by the *'the finger of God.'* Exodus 31:18.

This must have gone on for some time because the questioned was repeated. Eventually Jesus straightened up and said, *'if any one of you is without sin, let him cast the first stone.'* In this he sanctions the stoning. They were somewhat correct. Then he wrote in the dust of the ground again. He adds a moral caveat. Only the one's without sin can do this. That is, no one who has schemed in this case to cause the adultery to take place, or stood passively by while it happened, or brought this woman to me when similar things are in his own heart, can execute the stoning. That meant, nothing happened. According to our Lord's criterion, he was the only one who could have stoned her.

Jesus had sprung their trap.

Of course, the question that springs to mind is, 'What did he write?' Wouldn't you like to know? This is the wrong question. To understand what Jesus was doing we need to consider not what he wrote but where he was writing. He wrote in the dust of the ground. Obviously, what he wrote caused the accusers to leave the scene. It seems clear then that Jesus wrote down adultery and a whole list of sins of which the accusers were guilty. In this he displayed once again his knowledge of the secrets of men. In doing this, the accusers understood that they were as sinful as the woman they had brought before Jesus. Therefore, they left one by one. The woman remained. Where are you accusers? Has no one condemned you? No one sir.

Cast your eyes back to the dust of the ground. To the words that Jesus wrote. All that is needed now is a puff of wind, or even just the swirl of a garment as he stood up and the dust would be scattered and the accusing words would be gone never to appear again. That is what happened but they didn't get it, so he wrote again. Nicodemus and the Woman at the well, eventually got the heavenly meaning out of the earthly example, and in the same way the truth slowly dawned on this group.

This is the point, sins are sins, they offend God and man, but Jesus can wipe the record clean Then Jesus stood up and said, 'I don't condemn you either, go and sin no more.' Jesus hadn't come to condemn as we discovered when he spoke to Nicodemus. The woman was condemned already. The wrath of God was staring at her in the faces of the Pharisees. But Jesus had come to stay the wrath of God where there was a believing heart.

This event is also a demonstration of the kingdom of God. The question must arise, where was the man? The law of Moses, so crucial in the trap, in fact said that both the man and the woman should have been stoned. Leviticus 20:21. It demonstrated how the Law had been skewed to benefit men. It further shows that in the kingdom of God both men and women are equal. All have sinned and all can be redeemed.

We see a picture of a sinner in the hands of sinful men and then a sinner in the hands of the Sinless Saviour.

'Let him who is without sin'. The height of injustice is when we are being judged by someone who is guilty of the crime we are accused of. It goes to show, you cannot deal with the root of sin in man through a judicial system. In times gone by churches tried to deal with sins that people committed by applying a penal code. The Puritans executed people as witches when it was doubtful, they had anything to do with witchcraft at all. They made a woman who had committed adultery shave her hair and walk around with the letter 'A' around her neck, but the man was nowhere to be seen. Even today there are church organisations that if you do not do exactly what they want you will be cut off from the church and your family. Jesus did not put an 'A' around this woman's neck, he may have written one on the ground, but then he blew it away. John the Baptizer had given this testimony of Jesus, *'Behold the Lamb of God that takes away the sin of the world.'* The sin of the world is a warp in human nature that has passed down from one generation to another from Adam. It is what has separated us from God and given us the tendency to choose wrong over right.

The sins we choose to do can be dealt with judicially, but the root cause, separation from God can only be dealt with by the Sinless Saviour.

This is what this encounter shows us, Jesus who is able to take away the root of sin because he himself would pay the price for our sin by giving his life as an atonement for our sin. *'Where are your accusers?'* They looked around there was no one there. They looked at the ground, it was just dust, nothing was written there. 'Neither do I condemn you, go and sin no more.'

Therefore, there is now no condemnation for those who are in Christ Jesus, because through Christ Jesus the law of the Spirit who gives life has set you free from the law of sin and death. For what the law was powerless to do because it was weakened by the flesh, God did by sending his own Son in the likeness of sinful flesh to be a sin offering. And so, he condemned sin in the flesh, in order that the righteous requirement of the law might be fully met in us, who do not live according to the flesh but according to the Spirit.
Romans 1:1-4.

The wrong we do, we are responsible for, and we need to confess that to Jesus for him to take it away. But the state of sin into which we are born Jesus has taken responsibility for. That is why he went to the cross. All we have to do is acknowledge him as the one who has set us free form the life which walked ever further away from God, to a life that walks ever nearer to him. As Paul wrote later, 'In Adam all die, but in Christ all will be made alive.'

4. The Encounter with Mary at Bethany. 12:1-11.

The Background.

It is worth pointing out that this fourth encounter is also with a woman, but in this case there are several other people in close proximity. There are similar accounts in the other three Gospels; Matthew 26:6-16; Mark 14:1-11; Luke 7:36-50. Are they the same? It would seem that the Lucan account is of a separate event as it is placed in Galilee and John the Baptizer is still alive. Motivation for that act is recorded as gratitude. The other three accounts are placed just before the Passover at which Jesus would be crucified, and in the town of Bethany. Matthew, Mark and John describe the motivation for the act as, 'preparing for his burial' or words to that effect.

From this it can be reasonably concluded that Matthew Mark and John are describing the same incident, whereas Luke is describing something similar, but different.

Matthew and Mark describe the event as taking place at the house of Simon the Leper, (obviously a cured leper) John says it is in Bethany but does not specify at whose house. The presence of Lazarus, Mary and Martha suggest it was their house, but it could equally have been with a neighbour called Simon. It could be that Simon was the father of the brother and sisters.

The first anointing recorded in Luke, was an act of gratitude to Jesus for meeting the needs of a particular woman at a time of crisis in her life.

The second anointing at Bethany was an act of preparation for a time of crisis in the life of Jesus himself.

Some commentators say that it was the same Mary in both stories, and propose Mary of Magdala as the likely candidate. It must be pointed out however that the Mary in John's account had unrestricted access to the most valuable thing in the house and so she must have been the Mary of Bethany who could move around the house without arousing any concern. Unless of course Mary of Bethany and Mary of Magdala were the same person, a postulation put forward by some scholars.[16]

What we learn from this story is couched in the principle that a relationship with Jesus is a mutual experience.

This is not to say that actions of believers are in any way meritorious regarding their salvation, but that they are devotional, expressing the depth of love a person feels for the Saviour. As such they can be spontaneous, radical, mis- understood, effervescent and socially discordant, but like all acts of worship, if they come from a grateful and devoted heart, they are 'beautiful' to our Lord.

For vast periods of the history of the church the human response has been heavily curtailed by the prescribed litany. In the early centuries and later with the Moravians, the Wesley's, Whitfield, the Holiness Movement and the Pentecostal Charismatic expressions of the 20th century spontaneous and irregular expressions of worship were and are evidenced.

Christianity is to have a place for worship where the heart of devotion, adoration, and exaltation can be expressed. In

---

[16] **Dictionary of New Testament Theology. Brown.**

public worship 'a word from God is to be accompanied with 'a word to God.'

A person who speaks in tongues has no more any idea of what they are saying than Mary had of what she was doing, except something inside her compelled her to do it. It is the work of the Holy Spirit through the believer 'Glorifying Jesus.' 16:14.

Acts of adoration in worship can be intensely moving.

Mary was so moved she broke with convention and loosened her hair; she touched his feet; and she did not count the cost of her action.

Acts of adoration in worship can be prophetic.

'She did this in preparation of my burial.' As I have said, she probably had little idea of why she was doing what she did, she just knew she had to do it. Jesus gave the meaning of it. All acts of worship must be focused on the Cross and its implications. Matthew and Mark add this extraordinary caveat; *'Wherever the gospel is preached throughout the world what she has done will be told, in memory of her.'* Herein lies the mutuality of the Gospel, on the one hand it is Jesus and his cross and all that it means, and on the other side its Mary, representing all of us, with her oil, at his feet, and all that it implies.

Acts of adoration in worship can be life-changing.

'The fragrance filled the house.' Mary had poured the ointment on his feet and wiped it with her hair. She anointed his feet, and at the same time, through the same act, her head was anointed as well. The fragrance filled the house from the hair of Mary, not the feet of Jesus.

'You anoint my head with oil and my cup overflows.' Psalm 23:5.

Worship at the feet of Jesus elevates him to the highest place, Messiah, King of Kings, Lord of Lords, but the worshipper is elevated as well through the same process. Through the exercise of Holy Spirit prompted worship, Jesus is glorified and his glory fills the house and all who are present are elevated by the experience above the earthly realm, and bathe in the presence of the Almighty. When you come to worship, remember Mary and what she did, Jesus said you should.

The protest.

In the other gospels we see that it was not just Judas who protested at what was seen as a waste but all the disciples. This reflects the position that regards Christianity as a one-way street, all we have to do is obey a set of rules and follow a prescribed pattern of worship. Faith becomes a symbolic re-enactment of the gospel not a personal; relationship with Jesus.

We see Jesus, who is touched by the overflow of the heart of the believer.

Could not the value of the ointment be given to the poor?

This raises a deep ethical question still relevant today. When a new church building is erected; when a new person is taken on the church staff; when new equipment is purchased; and so on. Could not the money have been better spent?

The disciples did have a fund for the poor. Unfortunately, Judas was in charge of it, and used to help himself to its contents. John casts Judas as the spokesperson of the objection and discredits him by referring to the motivation behind the objection. There lies the principle here, the motivation. To give to Jesus out of a heart motivated by altruistic adoration is as essential as giving to the poor out of an altruistic compassion. In fact, one's giving to the poor is to be 'through the Cross.' It is with consideration of the God who gave, and the Christ who yielded up his life for us who have no means to repay him, that we re-enact the action of the Cross when we give to those in need who cannot repay. To give to those who cannot give back is likened to giving to Jesus himself. Matthew 25:31-46.

The giving of this woman benefitted no one at the time except Jesus himself. But it would eventually benefit the poor around the world because the event would be spoken of alongside the gospel. The principal of sacrificial giving would be taught alongside the principal of the worship of Jesus so that people would be enriched both spiritually and materially. The opportunity to anoint Jesus for his burial would happen once in the history of the world, the poor would be around every day. Deuteronomy 15:11.

We learn that the Jewish leaders began to plan to kill Jesus and Lazarus. That feeling of rejection weighed heavily on the heart of our Lord. In the midst of that gathering darkness, without instruction or coercion this woman anoints him. In our world which is increasingly hostile towards Jesus, his name blasphemed, his cause ridiculed, his people persecuted, his bible ignored, suddenly without provocation, someone whispers, 'Jesus, I love you,' that is a beautiful thing to him.

The Saviour is moved when his presence is appreciated.
This was a gathering in honour of Jesus. We have no right to his presence except he has bid us to come, and he has no obligation to come except he has promised to do so. It is one of the distinctions of Pentecostal worship that we have a place for the spontaneous response of people who feel that they just have to do something in response to the awareness of his presence. Adoration in words, song, tears, or the languages of the Holy Spirit, which are uttered as an explosion of the deepest emotions, cementing the fact that when his presence is a sensed a response is required.

The Saviour is moved when he sees a humble heart

Whenever we read of this Mary and Jesus, Mary is always at his feet, a sign of humility. Jesus is so much like us in every way, we could call him brother or friend, but we must never forget when we look upon his face, we see the face of God. Humility in his presence is that realisation of the greatest mystery of all, that God became man and dwelt amongst us. The hands that were nailed to the cross were the hands that put the stars in place. This moves the heart of Jesus.

The Saviour is moved when he sees personal sacrifice. Nothing we can do will ever compensate for or repay in any way what Jesus has done. But when he sees in us a heart of sacrifice that reflects the nature of his own heart, he is deeply moved. He sees that Christlikeness has come upon us. As Paul wrote later;

Philippians 2: 1-11;

> *Do nothing out of selfish ambition or vain conceit. Rather, in humility value others above yourselves, not looking to your own interests but each of you to the interests of the others. In your relationships with one another, have the same mindset as Christ Jesus: Who, being in very nature God, did not consider equality with God something to be used to his own advantage; rather, he made himself nothing by taking the very nature of a servant, being made in human likeness. And being found in appearance as a man, he humbled himself by becoming obedient to death—even death on a cross. Therefore, God exalted him to the highest place and gave him the name that is above every name that at the name of Jesus every knee should bow, in heaven and on earth and under the earth, and every tongue acknowledge that Jesus Christ is Lord to the glory of God the Father.*

5. The Encounter with Peter. 13:1-38.

This encounter, generally called, 'The washing of the Disciples' Feet,' took place at the event we have come to know as the Last Supper. It was a sort of transition between what the disciples knew as a Passover and what we know as the eucharist. It involves all the disciples but principally it is an encounter with Jesus and Simon Peter. It is Peter's reaction to the feet-washing that prompts Jesus to give the explanation; it is Peter's question about the betrayer that prompts the exposure of Judas; it is Peter's boast about dying with Jesus that prompts the prediction of his denial.
What it reveals about Jesus is no mystery as John makes it plain. **He showed the full extent of his love.**

The scene.
When we deal with the events immediately preceding the Crucifixion, we need to consider an issue that has run along just under the surface of the Gospel narrative all along but never been overtly addressed. That is the matter of 'Restoring the Kingdom to Israel.'

One like Moses. Deuteronomy 18:15. There was an expectation of the fulfilment of the promise that another deliverer like Moses would arise to emancipate the people from the oppression of Rome. The question was asked of John the Baptizer. 1:21. 'Are you that prophet?' Andrew's testimony in 1:41, was, 'We have found the Messiah,' that is, 'The Prophet.' After the feeding of the 5000 they exclaimed, 'Surely this is the Prophet.' It must be made clear that this concept of the 'The Prophet' was the concept of a Political Deliverer and restorer of David's Kingdom.
James and John, sons of Zebedee sought to guarantee themselves an elevated position in the Kingdom as they envisioned it. Matthew 10:21. Mark 10:35-37.

At the Passover meal they disputed who among them would gain the most important position in the Kingdom Luke 22:24-30.

Luke 22:36-38 was misunderstood to mean the beginning of the battle of deliverance.

Clearly Pilate had been led to believe by his informers this was a rebellion against the Roman State as his questioning seeks to establish this. 18:33-35.

Peter's statement in 13:37 implies loyalty in the envisioned battle for deliverance from Rome, not the cause of the Gospel. Jesus' reply is to say that at this time that will not be the case, but the day will come and then it will be for the right cause.

Acts 1:6. Even after the Resurrection the thought of Deliverance from Rome was utmost in their minds. In fact, it hints that all through the passion of Christ up until his death they expected some spectacular intervention that would begin the deliverance. Now on the summit of Olivet they sensed this was the last chance of their hope being realised and so they asked, 'Is it now, is this the moment?'

This was to some extent in the mind of all the disciples, but particularly Judas.

Enter the betrayer.

It seems clear to us as we read the Gospel narrative that Judas was always an outsider. However, he was involved in the early ministry. Matthew 10:3. When the Gospels were written down and commented on in hindsight, Judas is described as being in in a place of suspicion all along. (John12:6.)

I am inclined to believe that Judas passionately believed Jesus to be the Deliverer Messiah. He saw himself in a position of prominence in the coming Kingdom. He held the finances and he sat next to Jesus at the Passover meal. He was often engaged in errands for Jesus as a sort of agent. 13:21. No one thought anything of it when Judas left the group, meaning it was a common occurrence for him to be involved in some arrangement or other.

Clearly what Judas had in mind was to kick-start the revolution by engaging his contacts. 18:3. Judas was not too enamoured with the spiritual emphasis of Jesus. He wanted something tangible to be done to overthrow Rome. I believe that he fully expected, when he betrayed Jesus in Gethsemane, that it would trigger a response from Jesus to use his miraculous powers to deliver Israel. Of course, it did not. Neither did it happen before Herod, Caiaphas, or Pilate. Judas realised his error, fell into deep depression, found no mercy at the hand of the Jewish leaders, and so took his own life.

The evening meal.

We usually call it 'The Last Supper.' As Jesus sat with his disciples, he was acutely aware of what was in the heart of Judas and what he was going to do. 13:21-27. He was also aware that Peter would deny him for the same reason. 13:38. Peter had already removed himself from the front of the class to the back row as it were. It seems he was the last to be washed, and that he was so far away from Jesus he couldn't speak to him directly. 13:24

Jesus heard them talking about who would be the greatest in this Kingdom they were hoping for. All the disciples would desert him. Only John, from among the men, would be at the cross, and the practical help that would be required, was taken up by two 'fringe' disciples, Joseph and Nicodemus.

Jesus was aware he would soon return to the Father in heaven, and he was also aware of the pathway he would need to take to get there.

He also knew that he could escape it all and return to the Father unscathed. Matthew 26:53.

With that knowledge Jesus got up, took a towel and began to wash his disciples' feet. That was the full extent of his love.

By doing this Jesus revealed that his kingdom would come by taking the place of the servant not the place of the warrior, by serving the people not conquering them.

His kingdom would be in the hearts of people, not at this time a physical kingdom in the world.

They were going to struggle to grasp it all but he would see them through until the kingdom came in the power of the Holy Spirit.

Jesus loves without any guarantee of a response.

Judas was about to betray the cause, but he still loved him. Peter would yet deny, Thomas would doubt, they all would return to fishing, yet he loved them. There was no guarantee that any of the disciples would preach the gospel. He was going to the cross for the people of the world but there was no guarantee that anyone would ever respond to the gospel. When he called your name, it was never certain you would respond, but he loved you anyway in that he had already died for you. This was his mission, to stay the Wrath of God and to wrench the human race from the stronghold of Satan and sin, in order to give the opportunity to those who wanted to believe, to do so.

He went to the cross for those who would get it right first time; for those who would make a mess of it; and for those who would make a mess of it again and again. His love was unconditional love.

Jesus pays the price of love even though it could have been avoided.

He didn't have to take a towel to wash their feet. They could have remained dirty but he chose to do it. As we have noted, Matthew informs us that Jesus said he could have called on 12 legions of angels to set him free and take him back to the Father's side. (Matt 26:53) He would return to the Father, the glory he had before would have been restored, but he would have returned alone. There were no miracles here, no prophetic words of authority. Jesus chose Calvary and did not waver from his choice. He would be the atonement to pay the price for sin that had contaminated all humanity so that people would have opportunity to believe. He could have left us all with dirty feet, or more explicitly a sinful heart. He would have still been God. 'If you do not let me wash you, you will have no part in me.'

Jesus' love crosses social barriers

Maybe Jesus waited to see if one of the disciples would rise to wash their feet. It should have happened as they arrived. But no one moved. As Luke tells us they were pre-occupied with what positions they would have in the kingdom. '*I your Lord and Teacher have washed your feet so you should wash one another's feet.*'

That is not setting in place a ritual for Christians to follow, but something they should have done there and then. Each in turn take the place of the servant. They debated who would be the greatest but there was no contest to see who would take the towel. The highest office or status in Christianity is that of the servant. No one is too low, or too far, or too unclean, because the Master has already taken the lowest place, so whoever comes along can be served with the power and demonstration of the gospel. The Servant King came to establish the Servant Church.

Jesus love completely cleanses.

Peter first said that he couldn't let Jesus wash his feet and then said that Jesus should wash his hands and head as well. Thinking that washing the feet was insufficient. But you see it wasn't the washing that was important, that was just symbolic. What was important was the position that Jesus assumed. What he did in the lowest place is enough to cleanse any person who calls on his name at any time through the course of history. The love displayed at Calvary is enough to take away sin. Nothing needs to be added. These things are written so that you may believe, and in believing have life in his name. Salvation is not in any religious discipline; church ritual; doctrinal education; or self-discipline, as beneficial as such things may be. Salvation is by believing that what Jesus did on the Cross is sufficient for our salvation. By believing I am completely, utterly, and eternally saved, unless I do what Judas did and walked out of the presence of the Saviour, never to return.

Jesus' love remains as our example.
Our love must be without conditions. It is not our gospel. We cannot determine to whom it is presented and to whom it is denied. So, we present the Love of Jesus to all we come across. We must each take the servant role in relation to one another. No one is Lord and master. Luke 10:41-45. He who sits at the table today will serve the table tomorrow. Our love must be unwavering. The love of Jesus will cost. It will cost because the world in which we live denies the existence of absolute altruism, where something is done without thought of gain or reward. So, it starts with mockery and will move through the gears to persecution. But we are called like our Master to be 'sheep before our shearers, dumb, led as lambs to the slaughter. 'The love of Christ in us is the gospel, it need not be added to, it is sufficient in itself. Through these interventions by Simon Peter, John tells us, Jesus revealed the full extent of his love.

6. The Encounter with Mary of Magdala. 20:1-18.

This is the fourth woman in the personal encounters with Jesus that John has selected in order that we may believe. This is the first of the post-resurrection encounters.
We have touched on the identity of this Mary before. Mary, or Mariam, Miriam, or Mariamne seemed to be a very common

name at the time. The Gospels tell us of several, Mary, his mother, Mary wife of Clopas, Mary of Bethany, and Mary of Magdala.

Magdala was an important fishing and boat building town on the North Western shore of Galilee. This Mary therefore, was one of the women who accompanied Jesus and the disciples throughout his ministry in Israel. Luke 8:1.

This encounter reveals to us the nature of the ongoing ministry of Jesus to his disciples

It was early on the 1st day of the week before dawn, making it about 5 am, although technically the Sabbath ended at sunset on the Sabbath day. Mary and other women went to finish the burial procedure as it was incomplete on the day of crucifixion because of the beginning of the Sabbath. Clearly there was no expectation of anything other than attending the dead body of Jesus. John mentions only Mary of Magdala. The women had no idea how they were going to enter the tomb and negotiate with the guard that had been placed there. We have made a point of mentioning how the disciples expected some miraculous intervention on the journey to the cross, which never came. They were now observing the greatest miracle of all, but they didn't understand it because it wasn't the miracle they were expecting. It was a deliverance, but not the deliverance from the nation from Rome, but the deliverance of those who would believe from the tyranny of sin and death.

Mary's reaction when she saw the tomb was open was to go to the disciples and tell them, '*They have taken the Lord out of the tomb and we don't know where they have put him.*' We may ask, 'Who was meant by they?' It was almost as if she had been expecting foul play. The possible suspects were;

The Jewish leaders or the Roman soldiers.

We are well aware that in the matter of Jesus arrest these two groups combined. Their interests were the same. To have Jesus executed and the body locked away. The greatest problem from now on would be to contradict the disciples claim of resurrection. The matter would have been settled by producing the body. But as no body was ever forthcoming, it was obvious they didn't have it.

The disciples and the garden custodian.

There was obviously some link between these two as the tomb was owned by Joseph who obviously had access to the site and therefore knowledge of the custodian. The problem here is that Pilate and the Jewish leaders had thought of this and that is why the tomb was sealed and guarded. Matthew 27: 62-66.

Peter and John (on the principle of the anonymous disciple) rushed to the tomb to verify what they had been told. They made a more detailed investigation than Mary did. The tomb was indeed empty. But the grave clothes lay exactly where the body had been.

There are many more details of the next few moments in the other Gospels but we will confine ourselves primarily to the text of John.

Peter entered the tomb, left and went back to where he had come from, but said nothing. We don't know how it immediately affected him. John was different. He also entered the tomb, observed the same evidence and tells us that what he saw caused him to believe. What he saw was a personal pivotal moment in his journey of faith. He believed because he saw the grave clothes.

The circumstantial evidence.

The tomb was empty, the burial clothes were lying as if the body was still there, the head cloth was folded separately. There was no sign of forced or hurried activity. Something extraordinary had taken place but they were not quite sure what it was.

We can sometimes be so convinced that God should take a certain course of action, that when he does something differently, we cannot believe it is a work of God. We can see here the critical point that we must always consider when trying to decide if something is of God or not. What do the scriptures say? If the event we are considering is contrary to the spirit of the scriptures or the character of God, then we can dismiss it as not being a work of God, irrespective of the circumstantial evidence.

John makes sure we get the picture of the position of the grave clothes. These impacted him and brought him to belief. What did he see?

The cloth that covered Jesus was lying as if the body was still under it, just that it had fallen flat to the surface. The head cloth was folded separately. What John realised was that the tomb had not been ransacked or the body stolen. Everything was where he had been told it was placed on the Friday evening.

Much has been made of the 'headcloth lying separately.' It was called a sudarium. Literally it means a 'sweat cloth.' It was used to wipe the sweat from the brow of a working man. In the case of crucifixion, they were used to cover, and then clean the face of the victim if a burial was to take place. The face of Jesus would have been covered because it would have been hideously contorted after the torment of the crucifixion. When they got to the tomb the face would have been quickly wiped and the mouth and eyes closed. If there had been time it would have been more thoroughly washed. This headcloth was then placed separately by Joseph and Nicodemus when they laid Jesus in the tomb. This is what convinced John; nothing had been disturbed by the hand of man, friend or foe. If it had been disturbed the clothes would have lain haphazardly on the floor or would have been taken with the body.

When they referred to the scriptures, they would have looked at some of the following passages. Job 19: 23-27; Psalm 16:9-11; 30:8-10; Isaiah 56:5; Ezekiel 37:11-14. The disciples would add to this the statements they recalled of Jesus affirming that he would rise again. Matthew 12:39-40; 16:21; John 10:17-18.

Mary seems to have been left alone at the tomb.
She decided to look inside. There were now two angels in white seated on the burial slab of stone and they spoke to her. 'Why are you crying?' She repeated what she believed to be the case that the body had been stolen. Then she was aware of the approach of another figure who also asked her why she was crying. Through her tears she asked him if he had taken the body away as she assumed he was the man in charge of the garden. Then Jesus said her name, her eyes were opened and she realised who it was. It was Jesus. We can be re-assured that the shepherd knows his sheep and sheep know the shepherd. 10:14. She must have grabbed hold of his hands or feet, or threw her arms around him. Jesus did not say, 'don't touch me,'* there was no problem in touching him as we shall see, he invited Thomas to do just that. The text is best rendered, '*do not hold on to me.*'[17] Mary's attitude was, that she was never going to let him out of her sight again, ever. What Jesus was saying was, 'Don't try and draw me back into the way things were.' A greater and more significant day has dawned. You will continue to know me but not in the same way as you have been used to. I no longer just belong to you and the other disciples, but now I belong to the world.
The rendering '*My Father and your Father, my God and your God,*' is exactly the same in a broad spectrum of English translations. There is no more accurate reading that can exist to sharpen the meaning. I am going to my Father and my God. But you also can be with me, because he is your Father and your God as well. Go and tell the brothers.
This is an amazing statement, 'My God.' It is similar to the cry from the cross. Matthew 27:46.

---

[17] **Elliots Commentary**

In Matthew's cry from the cross the Hebrew/Aramaic is retained without translation, '*Eli, Eli, my God my God.*' His relationship with heaven as his body sunk into death was as a man to God, because he died in our place as a representative of all humanity. It was part of 'his humbling himself' that the link he had with heaven that was manifested in that moment, was man to God, not One equal with the Father. In fact, such a cry could have been on any dying man's lips.[18]

When 20:17 is translated back into Hebrew the phrase, 'Eli,' is not sufficient. Here one would require the term, 'Eloah.' (singular form of Elohim) It is still from the root word 'El,' the basic term for God in Hebrew but with a different ending. In the Greek the literal translation of Matthew 27:46 seems to be best rendered as, 'Thee of me.'[19] Whereas in 20:17 it is 'Theos' in Greek or Eloah in Hebrew, both which mean God the Majestic One.'[20] In Matthew he was conscious of slipping away from the nature of the ever-living God into the realm of death. In John he is ascending or approaching the Being of God once again. He was being clothed anew with, 'the glory I had with you before the world began.' 17:5. He was re-clothed with that which he laid aside in order to enter the realm of death. Philippians 2:8,9.

These remarkable words have a further implication. Jesus would return to heaven in the form of a man. This is made clear in Hebrews 2:5-11; 4:14; 9:11-15. Jesus as 'head of the body' which is his community of believers, is never-the-less part of that body. The High Priest was set apart from the people, but he was still one of the people. When he passed

---

[18] **Bible Hub.com**

[19] **Bible Hub.com**

[20] **Hebrew English New Testament. Society for the distribution of Hebrew Scriptures.**

through the curtain into the Holy of Holies, he was a man in the presence of God. Ephesians 4:16.

But he is also the first to rise from the dead and as such can take his place in the Godhead. Colossians 1:18. This brings us back to the prayer of John 17:21-24. That they may be one as we are one.

Mary reduced all this to the simplest, but still the most profound of statements, 'I have seen the Lord.' Mary had been broken hearted because she was still in the earthly plane. She was certain she had been separated from her Lord forever, or at least until the last day, Jesus had lifted her to see things from a heavenly perspective. He, now belonging to the heavenly realm, yet still knew her name, as she lived in the earthly realm. Jesus would rule and reign from heaven. He would intercede with the Father on behalf of his people on earth. He would appear at God's throne and also be present with his people on earth. They would still meet and converse, but not on the hills of Galilee, or the streets of Jerusalem, but at the Father's throne in heaven. It would not be only the disciples, but whoever called upon the name of the Lord. And wherever they would meet together in his Name, he would be there.

7. The Encounter with Thomas. 20: 19-29

This is the final personal encounter from John's selection. It is also set after the resurrection. It is placed immediately before the key verses; 'these things are written so that you may believe and in believing have life in his name.'

The account begins in fear and doubt but ends in the great confession of Thomas, *'My Lord and my God.'* This so profound and must surely rate alongside the confession of Peter, *'Thou art the Christ.'*

Jesus is revealed as one who has bodily risen from the dead. The showing of the wounds establishes that the post-resurrection appearances were not dreams, visions, or the appearance of an apparition. But Jesus had risen from the dead in his physical body. Thomas laid down the same criterion for himself.

This is clarified by the reference to Mary, 'don't hold on to me;' the reference to Thomas, 'reach out your hand and touch;' and later on Jesus prepared food for them to eat on the shore of Galilee. However, although he was a physical being, his physicality had taken on a new dimension in that he was no longer restricted by the laws of time and space. He could appear, disappear and pass-through solid objects. He is further identified as the same Jesus in that he bore the marks of the crucifixion and he knew them by name.

John wrote these things as it were saying, this is what we saw, this is what we experienced, this is what happened to us, as incredulous as it all sounds. It has been recorded so that you may believe. It calls for a belief that must supersede biology and the physical laws of the universe that usually apply. This supernatural belief is firstly focused on the person of Jesus but leads to a belief in the supernatural, in that we believe that Jesus can still work miracles in the lives of people today, through the power of the Holy Spirit.

The belief in the working of miracles today; the belief that Jesus will return to establish the kingdom of which he spoke and the disciples hoped; and the belief that Jesus will raise believers to life on the last day are all based alone in the belief that Jesus rose bodily from the dead. Paul wrote later, '*if Christ has not been raised, then our faith and preaching is in vain.*' (1 Cor 15:14)

John sees this as the culmination of all the things that he has written and so he places the key phrase immediately after this story.

This story reveals the nature of belief itself.

It is more than an intellectual understanding. John was not presenting evidence as in a court of law to convince a judge or jury that these were indeed the facts of the case and so a certain decision was inevitable. He was presenting his experiences and something of what it meant to him so that we may similarly experience the same thing and believe.

It is also more than a historical account. It is not a strict chronology of events. There is much that is not recorded. It is a series of events that draw one to the culmination of this account, that there is no other reasonable explanation than that spoken by Thomas, *'My Lord and my God.'*

It shows to us that the act of believing in itself is a supernatural experience. Without being able to answer every question, or explain every detail, something happens in the heart of man that causes a change to take place, so that he is raised from purely the mundane to a level of spiritual insight, that brings the confession so often repeated in the text, 'Lord I believe.'

It is taking the account of Jesus recorded as; incontrovertible, indisputable and authentic. Never modifying it; re-writing it; or re-interpreting it.

Jesus said to Thomas, *'Because you have seen me you have believed. '*

This was the final chapter of the revelation of Jesus. Nothing further would be added. He prepared them to receive the Holy Spirit in power in order to continue the proclamation of the gospel. Thomas symbolically represented all the eye-witnesses. Jesus said, 'you have believed because you have seen.'

As the representatives of the eye-witnesses, the confession of Thomas was the conclusion of the evidence of all those who had seen, *'My Lord and My God.'* It is the affirmation of where John started, *'The Word was God. We beheld his glory as the one and only to come from God.'*

Blessed are those who have not seen yet have believed.

Jesus now introduces the disciples to people of whom they, as yet, knew nothing. A people, of whose existence, they could barely comprehend. Those who have believed in exactly the same way, but never seen what they had seen. The experience of the one would be the same as the other throughout the centuries to come until it came down to us. Jesus prayed for us.17:20-26;

> *My prayer is not for them alone. I pray also for those who will believe in me through their message, that all of them may be one, Father, just as you are in me and I am in you. May they also be in us so that the world may believe that you have sent me. I have given them the glory that you gave me, that they may be one as we are one, I in them and you in me, so that they may be brought to complete unity. Then the world will know that you sent me and have loved them even as you have loved me. Father, I want those you have given me to be with me where I am, and to see my glory, the glory you have given me because you loved me before the creation of the world. Righteous Father, though the world does not know you, I know you, and they know that you have sent me. I have made you known to them, and will continue to make you known in order that the love you have for me may be in them and that I myself may be in them."*

We can expect that the impact on the eye-witnesses would be dramatic and life changing but here the power of the gospel is transferred to the record that eye-witnesses left behind for us. Their record becomes as powerful and life-changing as their experience. The written Gospel carries the same Holy Spirit anointing as the person of Christ himself. He was the Word.
'If you forgive anyone his sins they are forgiven, if you not forgive them, they are not forgiven.' 20:23.

In the power of the Holy Spirt each generation is charged to pass on to the next, two things.

1.   The unalterable and infallible record of the scriptures.

2.   The experience of belief of each generation.

In that process the gospel that is believed, communicated and testified to, will bring forgiveness on all who in the same way believe, but it will bring condemnation on all who refuse to believe.

Throughout the text of the gospel, John has taken pains to stress the power of belief and the consequences of unbelief. It is the same here, as they would transition from eye witnesses to non-eyewitnesses, belief would still usher in experiences of Divine power and grace, and unbelief would maintain the status of condemnation.

This text does not mean the disciples could randomly forgive or not forgive someone and that would be ratified by God. Jesus did not do that. He said, '*I say what I have heard my Father say and do what I have seen my Father doing.*' 12:44-50.

Jesus 'sent' his disciples just as the Father had 'sent' him. The sending of Jesus was not to condemn, unbelievers were condemned already. The 'sending' was with a message of salvation.

The continuity of the Gospel message and the continuity of the Holy Spirit ensures that the preaching of the gospel by the church will have the same effect as it did when Jesus himself was doing it. Some would believe and some would not.

The weight of responsibility is expressed by John in the pivotal verses which are found here. As we have said they are the key to the entire gospel. John was conscious that it had fallen to him to write an accurate account of what he had seen and heard and reflect what it meant to him, so that those who had never seen Jesus could believe and receive salvation.

CHAPTER 5.
SEVEN INTERACTIONS
WITH CROWDS OR GROUPS

John has selected a series of encounters for us to consider from the times Jesus conversed with crowds or groups. Most of them were hostile and largely deal with the people who chose not to believe. This reflects on the honesty of John's account as he does not seek to overstate the effect that Jesus had on the people with whom he dealt with. He makes abundantly clear the great blessings of salvation and the awful perils of unbelief. The subjects of the encounters do cross over in the sense that the same issues are raised again and again.

1. The Clearing of the temple. 2:12-23.

In most bibles this passage has inherited the title 'The Cleansing of the Temple,' The other gospels place the event in the last days of Jesus ministry and that is probably where it belongs chronologically. We have noted all along that John's gospel was a selection of events assembled to bring us to believe who Jesus was. They were not necessarily chronological. We may then enquire why John placed the story here near the beginning of his account. The reason is that it is a sequel to the miracle at Cana. It is a practical demonstration of that which was illustrated at the wedding.

When we spoke about the wedding, we saw how the fact the wine had run out showed the end of human effort. It illustrated that the regulated, ritualistic religion had run its course. What

Jesus did, showed what was to come would be miraculous and better than what had gone before. The Old was exhausted, the New was breaking forth.

The action in the temple was demonstrating the same theme, only much more dramatically. This brought Jesus face to face with the group called the Sadducees who governed the operation of the temple, the priesthood and the Sanhedrin.
They were wealthy aristocratic families who saw themselves as superior to the common person. Their haughty attitude comes through in the NT.
They emphasised the Torah, the first 5 books of the OT, to such an extent that they diminished the status of the rest of the OT. They rejected the extra biblical laws of the Pharisees. Religion to them was observance of rituals to obtain religious purity. The Torah had little or no bearing on the way they conducted their lives. Their faith was in the performance of the ritual not in personal conduct. They rejected all belief in the supernatural, which included the working of miracles and life after death. Politically they were supporters of the Roman occupation and tenaciously guarded their privileged position under the Roman authorities.

To use the title 'The cleansing of the temple' implies that Jesus was somehow restoring the temple to its proper use so that it could continue. By driving out the tradesmen he did make the point that the temple was supposed to be a house of prayer for all nations, and his zeal for that ideal. But it was only a demonstration, the tradesmen returned. There was a deeper meaning. A phrase 'Den of Robbers' is recorded by the other gospel authors. (Matthew 21:12-17; Mark 11:12-19; and Luke 19: 45-48)

This is a quotation from Jeremiah 7 9-15. This passage clearly tells, not of the restoration of the temple, but its destruction, and rejection by God of the religious procedures enacted there. While Jesus was driving out the tradesmen, the temple ceased to function, for an hour or so. This was prophetic of what would happen some 30 or so years later when the temple would be destroyed, never to be rebuilt until this day. They understood this because at Jesus' trial they laid the charge that he had threatened to destroy the temple and rebuild it. The tradesmen were only symptomatic of the problem. The Temple system was rotten to the core, not because of the business carried on there, but because the people who governed it had no heart for the things of God.

Then they asked what authority he had to do what he did. It was at this point that Jesus transfers the significance of the temple to himself. Jesus answered them, *"Destroy this temple, and I will raise it again in three days.'* This is what it reveals about Jesus.

From now on he would fulfil the ritual of the temple and be the means that man may deal with sin and worship God.

Matthew 12:6. Jesus said, *'I tell you that one greater than the temple is here.'* This was in a discussion about the sovereignty of Sabbath laws. Jesus was saying, sometimes the requirements of the Temple superseded Sabbath laws. Then he added, I am greater than the Temple and its laws, because I am the One to whom the Temple points.
They replied;

> *'It has taken forty-six years to build this temple, and you are going to raise it in three days? But the temple he had spoken of was his body. After he was raised from the dead, his disciples recalled what he had said. Then they believed the scripture and the words that Jesus had spoken.'*

His authority lay in the fact he had been sent from God to terminate the function of the Temple and replace it with his own act of atonement. After his resurrection, whatever went on in the temple would be futile, because he would be the mediator between man and God.

Everything that the temple had been built for would be embodied in Jesus and become the focal-point of the new way of worship.

- The Old had been a building; the New would be a person.
- The Old had been regulations; the New would be a relationship.
- The Old had been in one particular place, the New could be anywhere.
- The Old had been with repeated sacrifices, the New would be one once for all forever sacrifice never to be repeated.
- The Old was coming to an end, the New would last forever.

'My Father's House' would no longer refer to a specific building but could be applied to any place or people who would meet together in the Name of Jesus.

All the virtues the temple was built to dispense still apply; holiness; righteousness; mercy; forgiveness, atonement; justice; protection; but now they are to be found through belief in Jesus as the Son of God and the Saviour of the world.

A person could walk into the temple of old accompanied by the relevant sacrifice. They would observe the priest slay the animal aware that the animal was dying in their place. Then with appropriate confession of sin and acts of repentance, they could rise and walk out of that temple with a restored relationship with God.

Today we can come before Jesus our Lord and Saviour, guilty of sin and carrying the burden of shame, and with the prayer of confession and acts of repentance we can rise and walk away un-condemned and free of the guilt of sin, on the basis of the sacrifice of Jesus himself. The three principles of the temple are maintained, upholding the glorious Holiness of God; exposing the awful nature of sin; and the effectiveness of an atoning sacrifice. That is why it is called the New Testament or the New Covenant. It is the new set of promises by which we believe and approach the presence of God.

Jesus is the New Temple.
He is the meeting place between God and man. 14:23. Jesus replied;

> *Anyone who loves me will obey my teaching. My Father will love them, and we will come to them and make our home with them.'*

> *'That all of them may be one, Father, just as you are in me and I am in you. May they also be in us so that the world may believe that you have sent me.' 17:21.*

Collectively we are the New Temple.
> *'Don't you know that you yourselves are God's temple and that God's Spirit dwells in your midst? If anyone destroys God's temple, God will destroy that person; for God's temple is sacred, and you together are that temple.' 1 Cor 3:16;*

When we come together, we should display the awesome Glory of God; demonstrate the Power of God; and dispense the amazing Grace of God.

Individually we are the New Temple.
> *'Do you not know that your bodies are temples of the Holy Spirit, who is in you, whom you have received from God? You are not your own;' 1 Cor 6:19;*

This trilogy represents the way things are now. The dwelling place of God, the Most Holy Place, if you like, can be presented in its most simple form as the worshipping heart of a person. When many such worshipping hearts come together, we have a more complex or enhanced manifestation of God's presence. And when we come to Jesus, we have the ultimate manifestation of God's presence, because in him dwells all the fulness of God. Colossians 1:18-20.

The only visible presence of Jesus in the world today, is the presence of the believer. *'Christ in you the hope of glory.'* The Jesus that is seen is no more or less than the Jesus we believe in. Let us take care to reveal only the real Jesus

2. The discourse at the Feast of Tabernacles. 7:1-52.

This was the final stage of our Lord's journey hence it was taken with much care. From now on all that happened would be in or around Jerusalem.1-13. These verses relate to us the circumstances in which Jesus went up to Jerusalem for the Feast of Tabernacles. He went up secretly because he knew the Jewish leaders were waiting for him. In fact, it seems large numbers of people were waiting for him. Some of whom were eager to see him and others who were hostile and sought to do him harm. Jesus went to the Feast after 4 days. He did this not because he was afraid, but because he was conscious of God' timetable. 7:30. What an example this is of not being ahead or behind God's plan. But walking in step with his plan. If we are ahead of God, we can be ready for something, but the occasion is not ready for us. If we are behind God then the occasion may have well been set, but we were not there to play our part and an opportunity was gone.

The first thing is the Amazing Teaching of Jesus. 14-20.
His teaching in Galilee was extraordinary. But that was Galilee. It was not awash with scholars. The teaching here in Jerusalem was even more extraordinary because he was

amongst those who were the best expositors of the scriptures that Judaism could muster. He was un-schooled yet he was superior to them. This in itself was a miraculous sign. Jesus lets us into a secret. It is not his teaching at all. He got it from someone else. His Father in heaven. His Father sent him to speak to the people of Israel. The reason for this is that he does not seek to carve out for himself a place in Jewish academia, or stand in competition to the Jewish Leaders. His authority, like Moses, is that he is bringing something down from heaven. Jewish learning was couched in what one or another notable Rabbi had said about what God had said. Jesus words were simply, what God has said.

The second thing is again the sanctity of the Sabbath 21-24.

Although it is not explicitly stated, the healing of the man at Bethesda on the Sabbath still is an issue. They could not see that the Sabbath portrayed the perfect state in the Kingdom to come and was not an end in itself. No one could ever perfectly keep the Sabbath by making and keeping more and more laws. *'Man was not made for the sabbath.'* Humanity in its fallen state demanded things for its very existence that would break the Sabbath. Lame people would need to be carried; children would need nursed; rituals such as circumcision would need to be performed; donkeys would fall into pits and so on. Traditionally, things for the survival and well-being of all creatures superseded the Sabbath laws. So therefore, why could he not heal on the Sabbath?

The third thing, is Jesus the Christ. (Messiah) 25-36.

When the 'Christ' comes. We use the words Jesus Christ as if 'Christ' was his surname. The title 'Christ' is a Greek form of the Hebrew Mesiach, or Messiah. It means the 'anointed one, or one set apart for a specific task.' The people of Israel would never have used the word 'Christ' at that time but always the word Messiah. There had been several people called messiah in the scriptures. For example, David was a Messiah, and so were all the kings of Israel, because they were anointed. 1 Samuel 26:11. Cyrus, a pagan ruler, was called a Messiah. Isaiah 45:1.

There was also a hope in Jewish Theology for a great Messiah that was still to come. He was believed to be an ordinary human but with exceptional powers. He was equated with the 'The prophet' that Moses spoke of. Deuteronomy 18:15.

He would deliver Israel from her oppressors. Jeremiah 33:16; Psalm 72:11.

He would change the world order. Isaiah 11: 6-9.

He would be a remarkable leader. Isaiah 11:2.

He would have astonishing spiritual powers. Isaiah 11:4.

This is the sort of thing that was in the mind of these people as they discussed the claims of Jesus.

For those inclined to believe, their evidence was the miracles, and their hope for deliverance from Rome. For those inclined not to believe, his ancestry was a stumbling block, and the fact that if he was the Messiah, they would lose their positions of power and authority.

The reply Jesus gave was that according to their expectations, they did not know where he had come from. Ultimately, he had come from the Father. Neither did they know where he was going, for he was returning to the Father. A timid attempt to defend Jesus is tried by Nicodemus, but without much conviction and is abruptly shut down. 7:50.

The matter ends with insults, he was demon-possessed and a Galilean. Those who are convinced by the prejudice and bigoted viewpoint stated, he can't be the Messiah because he comes from Galilee and no prophet comes from Galilee. In that of course they were wrong. 2 Kings 14:25. Jonah came from Galilee and he was the prophet Jesus quoted as being the sign of his death and resurrection.

Reasons to Believe

The introduction of the Holy Spirit. 37-41.

The sum of these encounters was that the most vocal and influential of the Jewish Leaders had an inferior understanding of the scriptures; a distorted view of the Sabbath; totally mystified as to the identity of the Messiah; no idea about the Holy Spirit; and oblivious to where Jesus had come from. Their hearts were hardened and their eyes were closed to spiritual things; and they were missing the day of visitation. Luke 19:44.

We have had one or two references to 'The Holy Spirit,' but no specific explanation or who or what was implied. Here John gives the explanation that was not made at the time but was understood later. Amazingly the flow of the water was understood as referring to the Holy Spirit by the Rabbi's. [21]

The final libation offering had been made. This prompted Jesus to 'cry out.' That is, it was said in such a way as to gain attention of everyone present. It was not a quiet conversation. Isaiah 12:3. They sung these words, *'Therefore with joy will you draw water out of the wells of salvation.'*

The water was brought from Siloam and poured over the altar. It was no doubt referring to all the times that water had been miraculously provided to the people in the wilderness.

- The bitter water made sweet. Exodus 15:22-25.
- The water from the rock. Exodus 17:1-5.
- The water from the dry ground. Numbers 21:16,17.

In each case the water was supplied miraculously and the principal problem of their thirst was solved.

With this understanding Jesus said, 'If anyone is thirsty come to me.' Like Moses, I will give you supernaturally sourced water, but the water I will give will be a continuous satisfying stream. This reveals him as 'The Prophet' of whom Moses had spoken and they did not miss the allusion.

To receive this 'water' we must approach in belief.

---

[21] **Talmud tractate Sukkah**

'*As the scripture has said.*' This is difficult because there is no scripture verse that says this. We must bear in mind that the scriptures did not have chapters and verses as we do today. The only way to reference something was to say, 'Moses said, or Isaiah said.' Or as we have here, '*as the scriptures have said,*' which we must understand as a general reference to the overall tone of scripture, not to any specific passage. The one who is blessed of God will bless others.

Like the miracles that were reflected in the ceremony that sparked the comment, the Holy Spirit will so transform the believer, that from him will flow that which makes the bitter sweet, releases the blessing, and brings water to a dry land. Jesus returns to the subject of the Holy Spirit in further private conversations with the disciples which we will examine shortly.

3. Arguments over the Validity of his testimony. 8:19-59.

We return to the debates with the people and the leaders after the incident with the adulteress.

Where is your Father? The discussion around the Light of the World leads to the identifying of witnesses to validate his claims. They accept that he is a witness to himself. But who is your Father and will he bear witness to you?

The answers Jesus gave were deliberately obscure. This had to do with God's timetable for the acts of redemption as verse 20 explains. If he had been over-clear it would have hastened his death, he delayed it because there were still things to do.

You will look for me. The day will come when you will wish that I was back among you so that you could make different decisions concerning me. But I will be gone, and you will not find me. You will die in your sins looking for me.

This is so pertinent to us that when God calls, God visits, or God speaks, we are to be responsive and obedient. Gods plan of redemption is worked out in the finiteness of time. When it's time to go, its time to go. These people missed their day of visitation.

You are from below. You are concerned with earthly things. Which family you came from; how much learning you have done; how much power you have; how much wealth you have accumulated; and how well you can reason things out.

I am from above. You have no concept of the supernatural, of things beyond the scope of learning and the human sensations. The people that believe in me will share in the spiritual inheritance I have brought down from heaven, irrespective of who their father is or what they have learned. They will gain it by believing in who I am.

Who are you? This was asked to try and tempt him into the specific answer that would have hastened his arrest. Again, Jesus avoids their attempt to incriminate him.

Much to say in judgement. There is much more that can be said in judgment of you, but that is for another time. I can only say what I hear my Father saying and today is not the day of judgement. This they did not understand.

When you have lifted up the Son of Man. And we might add, and nailed him to a stake as did Moses to the serpent. You will be party to the act of crucifixion but then there will be a sequence of events beyond your control. There will be a darkened sun; an earthquake; a temple desecrated, without human hands; there will be a resurrection and an empowering of believers which you will be unable to counter.

Jesus speaks to those who put their faith in him. 8:30-31.
You must hold on to the truth to be free. The word 'free' struck a chord with the antagonistic Jews, not the believing Jews. We have never been in bondage! Oh really! Then what about Egypt; Babylon; Persia; Syria; and the Roman guard that was watching them at that very moment? All these were punishments on a nation that had turned from their Godly heritage. They were God's children because they descended

from Abraham. The Jew is advantaged in the things of God because they have a heritage that goes back to Abraham. The customs, history and language that Christian Theologians spend a life time trying to master, is at their fingertips from childhood. Yet, unless they believe in Jesus they are as lost as any gentile. That is because all inherited the disconnect between man and God introduced by Adam's transgression. And that makes them slaves to sin like everyone else. They may be children of Abraham, but they are also children of Adam. It is not Abraham that delivers us from the bondage of Adam's transgression, but Jesus, the Messiah.

A slave has no permanent place in the family. 10:34-40. He charged them with holding to faith in the ethnic descendancy not faith in God, as a basis for their salvation. They will lose their special status if they do not believe. Jesus stated, I am saying what I heard the Father say, because I was there when he said it.

He accused them of saying what their father has said, because they were there when he said it. Jesus has now introduced them to their spiritual ancestry, which will see means that the source of their unbelief is Satan himself.

This hits at the heart of Judaism and probably the general understanding of people today. The basis of Jewish belief on this matter is Deuteronomy 30:10-14. Here it is claimed that Moses made it clear that attainment of righteousness is possible by one's own righteous deeds. Condemnation falls through lack of performing righteous deeds. Paul however, knowing the argument, responds in Romans 10: 5-9. The word of faith is in your mouth to confess and believe the promises of God. There is no need to try impossible tasks of endurance to obtain righteousness (bringing Christ down or raising Christ up)

In fact, the Deuteronomy passage comes at the end of a long speech by Moses, where he foretells the many scatterings and re-gatherings of the people from the land they are about to enter. It ends with the verses that speak of a final restoration of the nation, when at that time the need for extraordinary efforts to obey God will no longer be necessary. It will only need a confession of faith. The extraordinary effort to deal with sin will have been achieved by the work of Jesus. It speaks of a day yet to come when the remnant of Israel will accept Jesus as saviour and Messiah. Romans 11:26.

The truth of the Gospel is that some of the blessings of that day can be known now through faith in Jesus Christ. That act of belief is to be the same for Jew and gentile.

John points out that the moral and spiritual failure of the people is evidence that keeping the law in its entirety is impossible, owing to the spiritual dominance they are subjected to.

We are not sinners because we do bad things, we are sinners because we are separated from God.

If you were Abraham's children you would display the characteristics of Abraham, that is faith towards the promises of God.

Children of the Devil. 8:42-59.

The Jewish understanding of Satan and Evil is very different from the Christian viewpoint. Judaism does not believe in a being called Satan or the Devil. But they do believe in evil spirits that influence mankind to do evil. The 'Satan' is the evil inclination in mankind.' [22] Judaism also teaches that God created both good and evil. Based on Isaiah 45:7 [23] some Jewish scholars have said that God is both good and evil. [24]

---

[22] **Everymans Talmud. A.Cohen**

[23] **This verse is part of the prophecy addressed to Cyrus. God is saying that the events that have brought him to the place if being Israel's emancipator were not a result of a battle of gods, as he would be inclined to believe, but all events, good and evil were created at the hands of the God of Israel. For this purpose, you are my servant. Benson Commentary.**

[24] Isaiah 45:5. As there is no 'other' beside God, then evil must have

In light of this, these statements by Jesus were startling and radical. Jesus is saying that the evil inclination has a source outside of man. Their position can be seen in their reply. '*You are demon-possessed.*' An evil spirit has dominated your inclination to evil, not a supreme evil being.

Jesus challenges them to point out any inclination to evil in his character that an evil spirit could possibly influence. 8:46.

Jesus points out that if they were from the same heritage then they would be in agreement. They are not in agreement; therefore, they are not from the same heritage. Jesus knows where he has come form and that he is saying what he has heard his Father say, so because they are saying the opposite, then their source of inspiration must be the enemy of God, Satan. This is not just an insult. Jesus gives three reasons why he has come to this conclusion.

The message of salvation is unclear. There are certain points of the gospel that are obscured when the Adversary has been allowed to dominate the human mind. They include;

- the fact that salvation has been obtained on our behalf by Jesus and all we have to do is receive it
- the wicked will perish.
- Jesus is the only way to God the Father
- and we are all sinners in God's sight and in need of salvation.

These things can only be clarified by the conviction of the Holy Spirit and thereby bring about conversion.

You would rather embrace death than life. The result of Adam's sin was the downward spiral of humanity and life in general on earth. Man was separated from God, and moral

---

originated from within him. Jewish virtual library. Good and Evil.

physical and spiritual degeneration set in. Anyone who courageously points this out is put to death as in the case of many prophets of Israel, the apostles, servants of Christ throughout the centuries, and increasingly more so by godless tyrants in our day. The main application of course, was he was referring to their plans for his own demise.

You would rather hold to a lie than the truth. Of all the lies that can be told there is one fundamental lie. These men had believed the fundamental lie. *'You will be as gods knowing good and evil.'* Genesis 3:5. This means, you will understand how to use good and evil to your intended purpose but not know the difference. You will not know when you are being prompted by the one or the other. Whereas God knows good and evil, but also knows the difference between them. The deception of Satan was to put something in the hands of mankind he had neither knowledge or maturity to handle.
The primeval lie was to doubt the command of God. The simple command needed embellishing, or explaining, or even modifying. A reference to the multitude of laws that had made the worship of God an onerous task. Jesus said, '*I tell you the truth.*' In other words, I am only saying what the Father has told me to say.

If anyone keeps my word, he shall not see death. This threw more fat into the fire. This idea of eternal life completely blew their mind. Abraham and the prophets were godly people but they died, yet simply by believing the words of Jesus you will not die? We are back to the demon-possession charge again. What makes you more powerful than Abraham?

Abraham saw my day. Genesis 22:18. In Hebrews 11:17 we are told that Abraham indeed saw the day of the resurrection of the dead. (i.e., My day) Jesus was before Abraham, and after Abraham. Jesus reveals himself as Eternal, possessing the essential nature of God. Those that believe in me will receive eternal life. That is a life that is conscious of the presence of the Eternal One in this life and in the life to come, just the same as Abraham.

You are not yet 50 years old. 50 was seen as the age of becoming an 'elder' and as such could give counsel and instruction. Jesus was in fact in his late thirties. [25]

They were saying you are not old enough to talk to us on such matters.

To sum up they had questioned the validity of his claims on the basis of;

- he was a witness to himself
- his father was not a notable scholar
- he was a Samaritan
- he was demon-possessed
- he wasn't old enough

Each objection was dismissed by the evidence our Lord presented. They had asked him, 'Who are you?' Now he told them in no uncertain terms, b*efore Abraham, I am.* This was the final hammer bow to their theories. The response to which was to try and stone him to death. Once again Jesus uses his Divine powers to bring the matter back into God's timetable and disappears from the scene for a while. Jesus reveals himself as not only the 'Son of God' but the 'Eternal Son of God'.

---

[25] **Based on the likelihood Jesus was born in 5 B.C. Matthew 2:1 He began his ministry in or around the 15th year of Tiberius Caesar which was 29 A.D. Luke 3:1 He had ministered about 3 years according to the 3 Passovers mention in John's Gospel 2:23; 4:43; 12:1 making the year of his death 32/33 A.D. and his age 37/38 years.**

4. Discourse on the Son of God. 10:22-42.

This next encounter was set at the Feast of Dedication or Hanukkah. This was the only feast to have no basis in the Hebrew Scriptures. It is centred around the lighting of a nine-light candelabra. It originated in the Maccabean revolt of 164 B.C. and is told in the book 1. Maccabees 4: 1:41-50; 2: 15-22; 4:36-59.

After the death of Alexander the Great, the middle east region had been divided between his four generals: Attalid was given Anatolia; Antigonid, Macedon; Ptolemy, Egypt; and Selucae, Syria. Syrian was now under the rule of the ambitious Antiochus IV who sought to force the region to follow the ancient Greek religions. He subdued Jerusalem in 167 B.C. and sought to eliminate the Jewish religion until our story begins in 164 B.C.

The Temple had been desecrated by Antiochus when he sacrificed a pig on the altar. A revolt against Antiochus commenced when a family from Modi'in near Jerusalem refused to submit to him. Eventually, when Jerusalem was liberated, the temple was considered unclean for Jewish worship and had to be cleansed. In addition to this story the Jewish Talmud recounts the account of the re-dedication. The special oil required for the seven-light Menorah was only sufficient for one day, yet it burned for eight days. This was considered to be a miracle and a sign from God that their cause was just. This led eventually to the construction of the eight-light plus one candelabra and the celebration of the feast of Dedication every year from on the 25th of Chislev for eight days, which translates to the second week of December. As Jesus attended this feast as recorded in John 10: 22 we must assume the story to be authentic. The ninth light was called the Shamash or 'servant light' was used to light all the other lights in turn over a period of eight days.

Are you the Christ?

The leader of the Maccabean revolt was Judas Maccabaeus. He was for a time regarded as a messianic figure because he delivered Israel from her oppressor. But his victory was short lived and soon the Romans would take over the region. The question is asked in this setting. The people are still looking for a politico-military figure. It could be that they were asking if this occasion of remembering a former deliverance would be the occasion for launching a new one. One can see the logic in it.

Jesus again affirms that he has made it plain who he is, but adds that their unbelief has clouded their understanding. He again alludes to the nature of belief as being a spiritual awakening that is independent of ritual practice and a simple observance of his miracles. Those that have been so awakened hear and see on a different level. They hear my voice and know who it is that is speaking to them. Jesus was saying he has not abducted these people from the house of Israel, but the God of Israel has awakened these people to believe in him. He will never abandon them but create with them a new household of faith.

I and the Father are One. This again is a provocative statement to Jewish ears, like the 'I am' we considered earlier. It goes to the heart of the Jewish confession of faith, the 'Sh'mah.' The Sh'mah means 'hear.'

The confession is, '*Sh'ma Israel Adonai Eeloheinu Adonai echad.*' Deuteronomy 6:4.

Hear O Israel the Lord your God, the Lord, is One. To the Jew this verse emphatically states that God is One. A unity, a singularity, without attendant or accomplice. Jesus was saying that he and the Father were of the same kind, just as he would say later, that he and the Holy Spirit were of the same kind. He is not saying that he is the Father, but that he and the Father are about the same business.

This results in another stoning attempt.

You are gods. The conversation now takes up the matter of Jesus being called the Son of God. Psalm 82:6,7 contains this statement.

> *; I said, 'You are "gods"; you are all sons of the Most High.'*
> *But you will die like mere mortals; you will fall like every other ruler."*

The context is that God is saying that the lawmakers of Israel are called 'gods' because they apply the law of God. Hence, they speak and act on God's behalf among the people. It was intended that their word would be God's word and their action would be God's action. Then, he argues, if that can be said in the Holy Scriptures of mortal men, then how can you object if I am called the Son of God. A similar verse is found in Exodus 7:1 where the Lord says to Moses, '*I have made you like God to Pharoah.*' Again, it implies that Moses was acting in God's stead, and if God himself had appeared, he would have done and said the same things.

As the 'Son of God' I am acting on behalf of God, and whether the Father was here or I am here the outcome of things is the same.

In these encounters Jesus has been challenged to reveal who he was, or who he thought he was. He has made it abundantly clear. He brings his answer to a climax with the use of the Hebrew sacred names that belong exclusively to God. 'I am' and 'One'. It could not have been put more clearer and the fact they repeatedly tried to stone him showed they understood what he had said, but they did not believe it.

5. The Entry in to Jerusalem. 12:12-19

This incident is recorded in each of the Gospels. Traditionally we celebrate this event on the Sunday before the resurrection and call it Palm Sunday. It was the week of Passover celebrations and it is recorded that over 2 million people would be present. [26] The Pharisees fear or claim that '*the whole world had gone after him*' was not that much of an exaggeration as it first appears.

The synoptic gospel writers place more emphasis on the selecting the animal for Jesus to ride on. John mentions it but focuses on the crowd and the response.

This was clearly meant to send a message to all who were observing, friend or foe. Jesus could have entered the city much more discreetly. But as we have seen the wheels to his destiny were well oiled by now.

Without doubt Jesus was revealing that there was about to be a clash of Kingdoms and he would emerge triumphant.

This crowd was marked by two distinct groups of people. Those who witnessed the raising of Lazarus and those who were visitors from other lands. By their words it was clear they thought they were watching the arrival of the Deliverer King.

The other gospel accounts tell us there were two donkeys, the mother and her colt. Jesus rode on the colt, while the mother donkey was not ridden. Matthew 21:1-9. The prediction of this was found in Zechariah 9:9.

Two things are significant here.

1. The older donkey represented the Old Covenant. It was not ridden because the domination of the Law was ending. He rode the 'new' or younger animal as a

---

[26] **Josephus.**

symbol of the New Covenant which was about to come into force by his death and resurrection.

2. He was going to enter Jerusalem on two separate occasions. To ride the mother donkey, he would signify that he was coming as the Delivering Conquering King. This was for a future time when he would set up the Righteous Kingdom at his second coming. Today he was entering as the King of Peace. He is coming to make peace between man and man, and man and God by the removal of sin. John notes that the significance of these things was only understood after his resurrection. No doubt explained by Jesus. Acts 1:3.

Hosanna. Blessed is he who comes in the name of the Lord. Blessed is the King of Israel. Matthew 21:6-17. This is quoted from Psalm 118.25,26. It is one of the clearest Messianic statements in the prophets.

In modern worship songs the word 'hosanna' has become a word of praise and is often used as an equivalent to 'Hallelujah.' Hosanna was not in its original usage a praise word. It means 'Lord save us now!' The shouting of the children was not an innocent adoration, but a repetition of the 'deliverance' cry of the crowd. Hence the indignation of the Leaders.

The one who comes in God's Name, has come from God to redeem Israel.

'Baruch haba b'shem Adonai.' Blessed is he who comes in the Name of the Lord.

And if we needed any further clarity, we have it in the next phrase, *'The King of Israel.'* There was no doubt in the minds of these people that they were witnessing the Messiah entering Jerusalem to deliver Israel.

They laid Palm branches on the road for him to ride over, and waved Palm branches at him. This was not a Passover custom of any kind. It was something that belonged to another feast, the Feast of Tabernacles. Part of the significance of that feast is the coming of the King to establish his Kingdom and Palm branches are waved to signify it.[27]

By doing what he did Jesus brought the whole thing to a head. This was a four-way conflict of Kingdoms.

- The political arrangement as it was, defended by the Jewish Leaders and the Romans.
- The kingdom the crowd had in mind, the restoration of the Kingdom of David.
- The Kingdom Jesus had in mind, the Kingdom of God that brought salvation.
- The Kingdom of Darkness which sought to annihilate the Saviour of the World.

Only one would emerge triumphant. The scene was set. In just over thirty years' time, the fate of Israel as a nation would have been sealed for that time in history. In less than a week the crowd would be disillusioned. By the beginning of the next week Satan would have been dislodged from his dominance over human hearts. Jesus would have risen from the dead and declare, *'I am the Living One. I was dead but behold I am alive for evermore and have the keys of death and hell. Revelation 1:1*

6. The Interview with the Greeks. 12:20-36.

A group of Greeks desired to meet with Jesus. The term 'Greeks' may not specifically refer to men from Greece, but refer in general to gentiles. They had come to Jerusalem for the feast. Like many gentiles of that time, they had found an emptiness in the paganism of Greek and Roman culture and

---

[27] **Jewish Encyclopaedia**

had turned to the God of Israel. Historically they became known as 'God-fearers.' We read about them in the book of Acts. [28]They became the first Christian Communities. The encounter prompted quite a response from Jesus which revealed something further about him.

The hour has come. The process that would lead swiftly to his crucifixion, burial, death, and resurrection had irreversibly begun and it had been somehow triggered by the encounter with these gentiles. This hour would 'glorify' him. That is, it would be the series of events by which he would be renowned above all other, for all time. Indeed, Paul later summed it up by saying, *'We preach Christ Crucified.'* (1 Cor 1:23.) It remains that, 'The Cross,' by which we mean the events of the trial, death, burial, resurrection, and ascension of Jesus, is the core of Christian worship and teaching.

Almost entirely, Jesus' ministry had been confined to Jewish people. However there had been hints that his kingdom would spread beyond the Jewish nation, but the disciples did not really grasp that. Indeed, the debate is well documented in the book of Acts. There was a hint as far back as the birth of Jesus, that he would in fact be more than the King of the Jews. The visit and adoration of the Wise Men, gentiles from eastern lands indicated his ministry would spread beyond Israel,

This is the revelation of this encounter. **Jesus would not only be the Messiah of Israel, but the Saviour of the World.**

Jesus spoke of the continuous regeneration of the seed of the gospel. Firstly, he was the gospel. Grace and Truth came through Jesus Christ. The disciples had participated in ministry themselves as we are told in other gospels, but it is not part of the gospel story. The gospel story is exclusively

---

[28] **Jewish New Testament Commentary. Stern. Acts 10:1; 17:4; 17:1`7; 18:7.**

about Jesus, what he said and did. But Jesus said this was only a single seed, Jesus and Jesus alone. Everything was done by him. But if that seed dies it will produce many more seeds, and so on, it would continue to reproduce. This is how the gospel would reach the world. Through their process of belief in what they had witnessed they would be empowered to do throughout the world what Jesus had done in Israel, and so it would be passed from generation to generation.

Now is my soul troubled.

This reveals to us what went on in the heart of Jesus when he contemplated the cross. Looking back from our vantage point, we tend to embellish the cross and almost make it something beautiful. But here we see that from our Lord's perspective, the cross was terrifying, ghastly, and foreboding. Its dark shadow fell across his soul as he faced the gentiles knowing for them to believe, his death was near and he would die for the sins of the whole world. The thought even flashed though his mind, *'shall I ask the father to save me from this hour?'* Then the temptation was dismissed, *'no, it was for this purpose that I have come.'*

Further Jesus was troubled because this would be the moment when mankind could no longer hide in ignorance of what God required people to do. He had always alluded to the fact that belief would save and unbelief would condemn. Now was the critical moment, the once for all, forever offer of salvation would cut through humanity like a knife, both Jew and Gentile, millions would believe, but millions would not believe and live their lives, and face eternity under the wrath of God. This troubled him. In Acts 17:30 we see Paul alluded to this when he said in relation to idolatry, *'In the past God overlooked such ignorance, but now commands everyone everywhere to repent.'* What had been largely a matter for Jewish people was now the concern of the entire world.

The voice from heaven. This is so significantly important. The whole ministry of the Gospel began with a voice from Heaven. *'This is My Son.'* Matthew 3:16.

Supernaturally God spoke from heaven to confirm that Jesus was in fact who he claimed to be. Firstly, God said it as a witness to the Jewish people. Now it was said for the people of the world, whom, in this case, Jesus elevated these Greeks to represent. Jesus said this was not primarily for his benefit but for the purpose of the gentiles to whom he spoke. They heard the supernatural confirmation so they became eyewitnesses of the ministry of Jesus. They came to see what Jesus was about, but this was no casual enquiry, they saw and heard something that demanded they believe or reject what they had experienced, they could not ignore it. If they reject Jesus, they reject the voice from heaven. In this they were commissioned to the same level as the Jewish disciples were.

The judgement of this world. What Jesus was saying was, now the event is approaching by which the whole world will be judged. Whether or not people believe that Jesus died and rose again for their sins, they are judged, nevertheless, on this event. Accept and be saved, reject and be lost. The criterion was not if we had observed religious ritual, or even kept the ten commandments, but how have we responded to the death and resurrection of Jesus.

The prince of this world. This refers to Satan, the adversary. It reveals to us that the Cross of Jesus was far more than a physical event. We are familiar with the nails, whip, thorns, spear, the abuse; but that was just what happened on earth. The Cross was a spiritual battle against satanic and demonic forces. The struggle of the spiritual was far more intense than the struggle of the physical. Peter alluded to it in '1Peter 3:18. *He was put to death in the body but made alive in the Spirit through whom he also went and preached to the spirits in prison.'* Paul in Colossians 2:15. *And having disarmed the* *powers and authorities he made a public spectacle of them triumphing over them by the cross.*

This is the darkness that John wrote about in chapter 1. The darkness that made it impossible for mankind to believe. Jesus penetrated it with the light of his presence and now Satan would be driven from his place of authority so that whosoever called upon the name of the Lord would be saved. *'Put your trust in the light while you have it so that you may become sons of light.'* Wherever you go with the gospel my light will become your light and people will believe.

When I am lifted up. This goes back to image of the snake on the stake presented to Nicodemus. So, the Son of Man must be lifted up. This statement reveals the cross. The lifting up on the cross was to make a spectacle of him, but the lifting up was also indicative of the ascension. Man lifted him up to die, God lifted him up to reign. The ascended Christ will reign until all his enemies are under his feet. And whoever lifts their eyes to the crucified saviour and then the ascended Lord in belief will be saved.

The Lament of the Prophet. 12:37-50.
John turns again to the perplexing matter of unbelief. The unbelief of the Jewish people is cast against the belief of the gentiles. The hearts of many of the observers of his ministry stood in a spiritual state of unbelief. They had such entrenched views about God, religion and the Messiah that they had barricaded themselves off from God. No matter what Jesus said or did, they would find some reason not to believe. As far as they were concerned, the God they served, and the Messiah they hoped for, could not possibly say and do what Jesus said and did. There are those hearts throughout the ages who have convinced themselves that the gospel is a lie, propagated by deranged people, making unsubstantiated claims, to the extent they will not stir themselves to investigate

the matter. *'Who has believed our report and to whom is the arm of the Lord revealed.* Isaiah 53:1

The lament of the prophet has found its fulfilment again. God has displayed his might and power once again, but the people have not believed.

The second quotation is from Isaiah 6:8-10. It is part of the commission of Isaiah himself. What Isaiah faced; Jesus faced. Eyes that see not; ears that hear not; hearts that understand not; and spirits that turn not.

Isaiah saw Jesus' glory. Isaiah had this extraordinary vision of the glory of God. Isaiah 6:18. Three things stand out in these verses. The Glory and majesty of the Lord; the sinfulness of man, and the need to proclaim the call to repentance. That is what links this to the ministry of Jesus. A God of holiness is concerned with men of sinfulness.

John adds here that there were some who believed, but secretly, for fear of the Jews. They loved the praise of men more than the praise of God. It seems that this was not a permanent state because some who were obscure at this stage of the story, become pivotal characters later on.

Like Isaiah, symbolised by the burning flame that touched his lips, Jesus could only speak what he heard the Father say. As the light Jesus shines God's grace on all. Yet those who choose unbelief reject the saviour and the One who sent him. To reject his word means to render them of no value or significance. It is saying the revelation of the Glory of God was nothing more than the rantings of a deluded man. Rejecting Jesus will be the touchstone of the final judgement.

Jesus makes clear the two sides of the gospel message. It will save and condemn depending whether it is believed or rejected. He reminds us that there is no condemnation from him at this time, but the word that fell on deafened ears will be a witness at the final judgement. Here Jesus reveals himself as the judge.

7. The re-commissioning. 21:1-25.

The final group encounter of John's gospel reveals Jesus as the Lord of restoration. I don't think we fully realise the utter devastation the disciples suffered, their world and their faith were shattered. They had risked everything to follow Jesus and now it seemed to have been a hoax. The Miracles of deliverance for which they had hoped had not materialised. Judas had betrayed all of them, Peter had denied he knew him. None of them had the courage to step forward to bury his body, that was done by Joseph and Nicodemus. They had disbanded as only few were at Galilee. They had fled to Galilee because they were afraid of the Jewish leaders. His appearances to them convinced them of his resurrection from the dead, but did not explain why he had not liberated Israel from Roman occupation and even now was doing nothing about it.

Easter 'Fridays' happen to all of us. It's not that we cease to believe in Jesus but that we have had hope destroyed. Like these disciples we were convinced things were going to work out in a certain way, but they did not. As things wound down to the Cross, they were sure that there was going to be a divine intervention and all would be changed. But it didn't happen. No kingdom appeared. Evil triumphed. There was no healing, no answer, no deliverance. Easter Friday people became Easter Saturday people, hope gave way to despair. The two disciples journeying to Emmaus clearly illustrate this, *'we had **hoped** he was the one who was going to redeem Israel.'* (Luke 24:21)
Jesus knew that a feature of the 'not seeing but believing era' would be disillusionment, when things would go in an unexpected direction. So, he reveals himself as the Lord of Restoration.

The Appearances to the disciples.

The disciples were still in fear of the Jewish leaders. They probably thought that if that is what they can do with Jesus what hope is there for them. Only 4 of the original 6 are there. Not only did they consider themselves failures in the ministry Jesus had given them, they were now inept at fishing as well. Jesus had appeared to them, but he was gone again and things remained the same.

We need to appreciate what a giant leap it was for these people to move from the period of the eyewitness to the period when Jesus would not be physically present.

We begin with no Jesus, no hope, and no fish.

The catch of fish.

Jesus said cast your net on the other side, they did and caught an enormous catch of fish for the size of the nets and the boat they were using.

In this process of restoration Jesus taught several things.

He was still the author of miracles. He was restoring to them the power to walk in the miraculous. There would be nights of weeping but also mornings of joy. They would never be able to fulfil their task of taking the gospel to the world in their own strength and skill.

They were reminded that the realm of the miraculous was to bring people to recognise Jesus, not to bring about a political revolution. When they caught the fish, they recognised Jesus. They were to prepare spiritual food for the world as Jesus had prepared breakfast for them. The breakfast was made up of the fish Jesus had and the fish they had, meaning, the kingdom God would be made up of the people whose lives Jesus had influenced directly and the lives he would influence through the ministry of the disciples.

When you were young, when you were old.

This was probably written when John learned of the death of Peter and that had brought these tender moments to mind.

When Peter was young, he had dreams and ambitions for his life and future. As we have seen, he predominantly longed for the restoration of the kingdom to Israel. But when he was old, he would not see this dream. He would be led to an Easter Friday of his own. This is not what he had desired to do, but what Jesus has called him to do, follow me. Peter went willingly, to prison, he was the first who went to the gentiles, he went through Asia and ended up in Rome. Jesus restored him to the apostolic calling he had bestowed upon him. As he approached his death he had written, *'We did not follow cunningly devised stories when we told you about the power and coming of our Lord Jesus Christ, but we were eyewitnesses of his majesty. (2 Peter 1:16)*

Then Peter said, " what about John?' He also had dreams and ambitions. Peter, it's none of your business. If John never has an Easter Friday that is up to me. Follow me.
So, the restoration was complete. Most supremely their eyes were lifted up to new dimensions. Never again would they see things from an earthly perspective. Their vision was to be the world beyond Israel. The power was to be in his name and on his behalf. Their task was to prepare spiritual food for people. Maybe you need restoration today. Are you in the confusion of easter Friday, or the despair of easter Saturday? This final revelation of Jesus in the gospel of John shows Jesus as the Lord of Restoration. He will lift your outlook from the narrow view of what went wrong to the broad vision of your place in his plan of world redemption.

CHAPTER 6.
SEVEN INCREDIBLE
STATEMENTS

These are the seven Great sayings of Jesus declaring who he was by the use of the clause, 'I am.' The clause would not be lost on the ears of his Jewish audience. They were the words of the sacred name of the God of the people of Israel. Never spoken or written. Yet the words flow freely from the mouth of Jesus.

We have seen that there is an eighth 'I am,' without an appendage. John 8:58. *'Before Abraham was born, I am.'* This makes it clear to us that they got the message. Before Abraham was birthed on this planet, I forever existed. This is not a 'Christian reading back into the text a significance that was never there.' They understood it because they picked up stones and intended to kill him for using the Divine Name and claiming to be God.

This is probably the most profound of statements, summing up the seven we shall consider. We are introduced to eternity. A concept beyond human comprehension.

It comes from the revelation of God to Moses. Exodus 3:14,15. This was startling and shocking to the people. It was no slip of the tongue, Jesus said it seven times with a different appendage.

In the words of the old hymn.

> *Immortal invisible, God only wise, in light inaccessible*
> *hid from our eyes, most blessed most glorious the*

Ancient of days, Almighty victorious thy great name we praise. [29]

What is the sum of these statements? **It is the Personalising of Religion.**

Christianity is essentially a relationship with Jesus. We are not guardians of ritual propagating a particular way of worship or defenders of truth condemning all who dare to differ, we are people in a dynamic relationship with Jesus the Son of God, the Saviour of the world. That relationship alone determines our avenues of expression in worship; our standards in society, truths to which we hold dear, and the direction in which we travel. It is all about Jesus. We hold the bible to be the word of God because it tells us about Jesus; we partake in communion because it tells us about Jesus; we love our neighbour because Jesus did; and we will not deny the faith because Jesus didn't.

'I am,' not anyone else. We live in a world where everything and everyone must be included. But Jesus stands alone and unique.

It is not like saying 'I am the prime minister.' He was voted in and can be voted out. It is more like saying 'I am the Queen.' It was pre-ordained for life.

'I am' - not you. We are not self-saviours. Its more than my journey, or what seems good to me. It's not lifting myself up in grandeur or crushing myself down in failure. We enter his kingdom not by what we have done or not done, but by what Jesus has done. We are what we are by the grace of God.

1. I am the bread of life. 6: 35.

This naturally follows on from the great sign of the feeding of the multitude. All the other statements are a consequence of

---

[29] W Chalmers Smith **Redemption Hymnal**

this one. 6:35; Then Jesus declared, *'I am the bread of life. Whoever comes to me will never go hungry, and whoever believes in me will never be thirsty.'*

Each of the statements reveal the same meaning. Our blessings at his expense. There is no salvation, no gospel, no relationship with God except that bestowed on us at the expense of Christ himself.

The discussion falls into three parts.

Firstly, the discussion centres around the multitude who witnessed the miracle. 6:25.

This crowd had meticulously deduced where Jesus was, not because they had seen through the sign to the Saviour, but because they wanted to watch him make more food with which to feed them. They appreciated what he could do but had little or no interest in who he was. John was making it clear to his readers that to believe in Jesus was no easy matter even when they had seen him face to face. This is because it did not only depend on who Jesus was, but also what was in their heart. And on this point, they were sadly lacking. He charged them simply with wanting entertainment. Jesus then contrasted the food which needs replenishing, and food that is eternally satisfying. He was charging them with misplaced effort.

'What must we do to do the works of God?' It was really saying, what religious ritual do you suggest will gain us the sense of spiritual satisfaction you are talking about.

He made it clear that he would dispense this spiritual satisfaction as the Father had authorised him to do so. Therefore, the only viable work that they could do was to believe on the One whom God had sent among them.

Then the demand was, as usual, demand for authentication. If you want us to believe you must show us a sign. Moses did it with the Manna, can you do anything like that?

Many comments at this point become incredulous. Had they not just seen a miracle? Was that not good enough? But let's be fair. There was a crowd of 5000 men and who knows how many women? Jesus did not distribute the food. His disciples did. Only those near to Jesus would actually witness what he was doing. Those towards the fringes would get the food but would not have seen what happened, maybe they never bothered to find out. So, they asked to see an observable sign.

Moses and Manna. Jesus points out that Moses did not supply the Manna but God did. As the Manna came from heaven, so had he. The loaves and fishes were not God's gift, he was. Jesus places himself at the centre of human need. To receive that spiritual satisfaction they were longing for, they had to believe on him, whether there were signs or not.
Jesus then sums up the matter with a series of statements we can put something like this;

- He who comes to me will never be hungry or thirsty.
- Those who come to me will be motivated by their belief in who I am.
- Those who come on this basis I will never drive away.
- I will raise them up in resurrection on the last day.
- This is the Father's will.

Secondly, the discussion is focused on the Jews. 6:41.
It seems that this discussion had now moved from the outdoors to the synagogue in Capernaum. We can assume that by 'the Jews,' Jewish leaders are meant.

Jesus said to them,
'Truly I tell you, unless you eat the flesh of the Son of Man and drink his blood, you have no life in you. Whoever eats my flesh and drinks my blood has eternal life, and I will raise them up at the last day. For my

flesh is real food and my blood is real drink. Whoever eats my flesh and drinks my blood remains in me, and I in them. Just as the living Father sent me and I live because of the Father, so the one who feeds on me will live because of me. This is the bread that came down from heaven. Your ancestors ate manna and died, but whoever feeds on this bread will live forever.' 6:53-59.

What does this mean? In 1 Chronicles 11:19 David was in the Judean desert and expressed a desire to drink of the water from the well at Bethlehem. His soldiers took it literally and went in risk of their lives to get the water for him. When they brough him the water, David says, *'Far be it from me, O my God, that I should do this! Shall I drink the blood of these men who have put their lives in jeopardy? For at the risk of their lives they brought it.'*
He says that to drink this water would be like drinking the blood of these men, not literally their blood, but it would be like profiting from their near death, since they risked their lives for him. You could say, enjoying the benefits which came at the expense of risk to their lives. That phrase really sums up what Jesus is talking about here. When He refers to eating His flesh and drinking His blood, He is talking about enjoying the benefits which come from His death. The blessings which were his, and his alone, achieved through his flesh and Blood are shared with those who believe in him, that is eating His flesh and drinking his blood. That is the Bread of Life.

Thirdly the matter is discussed with the disciples. 6:60.
We could have anticipated that the previous groups of people would not take kindly to what he had said. But when we turn to the disciples, we would expect a more favourable response. But that is not so. Of course, this is not referring to the twelve. They and others remain. But many leave.
Jesus' revelation here is so important. In order to believe and follow Jesus there has to be an 'awakening' in the heart of a

person in order to believe. If this awakening is stifled or not allowed to stir through, prejudice, unbelief, or dis-interest then that person may as well go home. They will never come to a point of belief in who Jesus is. As a result, the disciples grumbled, 'this is a hard teaching.' And so it is.

No one can come unless the Father enables him.

Jesus turns to those who remain and says to them, *'You do not want to leave as well do you?'* To which Peter replies, *'Lord to whom shall we go? You have the words of eternal life. We believe and know that you are the Holy One of God'* That is the confession of an awakened heart.

Jesus closes the discussion with the shattering words, *'I have chosen you twelve, but one of you is a devil.'* John tells us on reflection that this was Judas.

This is quite remarkable. Jesus was saying that even the twelve were not safe from deception. The word 'devil' emerges from the Greek 'diablos' and can be paired with the Hebrew 'Satan.' It simply implies an adversary, or, 'the one who is against.' Jesus tells us in 8:44' that those who refuse to believe have a sort of spiritual ancestry to the devil.

'Iscariot' probably indicates where Judas was from, a town in Judea. That makes Judas the only disciple who was not from Galilee. We have contended throughout these studies the point of view that Judas was disillusioned with Jesus' emphasis on a spiritual kingdom, and tried to put him in a position where he would use his supernatural powers, to trigger a political rebellion. When this failed, Judas, full of remorse, took his own life.

Throughout this chapter the emphasis returns to the matter of motive. Why are you following me? The only motive that will stand the test of time and circumstance is when God has awakened the heart to believe and that awakening is not contaminated by other agendas. As Peter put it, we have no one else to turn to.

In each of the following statements, the declaration is stimulated by what was going on at the time.

2. I am the light of the world. 8:12.

These words were uttered in the Temple Courts. 8:20. It seems certain that these verses are a continuation of chapter 7, and therefore we are at the time of the Feast of Tabernacles.7:10. We know that during the feast many candelabra were lit in the Temple Courts to illuminate the evening festivities. Doubtless this was a remarkable scene which prompted Jesus to say these words. Two things were signified by this, one, the remembering of the 'Shekinah' light that illuminated the Temple of old and was the presence of God himself (1 Kings 8:10-11); and the Great Light that was to come which indicated the Messiah. (Isaiah 9:2).
At some time during the celebrations Jesus spoke out and said as it were, 'I am the One to whom this symbolism points.' [30] When I am here, God's presence is here; when I am here the Messiah is here. I am the 'Shekinah.'
All the feasts of Israel pointed to the day of the righteous Kingdom of the Messiah. Jesus was saying as long as I am here that Kingdom is here. The blessings of the Kingdom will not be established permanently until Jesus returns, but some things of that Kingdom can be found in the community of those who believe. Particularly the Presence of God. (Matthew 18:20) Light, in particular, emphasises that God is Present. Those that follow Jesus walk in the daily awareness of the Presence of God.
The response was threefold. Some religious people rejected Him 8:13, others were inquisitive enough to ask Him for more information 8:25, and still others believed and received him 8:30. The joy associated with the lights and water rituals of the

---

[30] **Dictionary of New Testament Theology Volume 3.**

Feast of Tabernacles anticipated Jesus' coming and bringing light and life to a dark, sinful world.

He alone penetrated the darkness of unbelief. We are to be lights in this dark world, but the light is not anything of us, it is Christ in us, the hope of glory. Only by total dependence in the light that overcame the prince of darkness can we shine a light in our generation.

3. I am the gate for the sheep. 10:7-10.

This claim and the next one are both in response to the previous incident in chapter 9. The expulsion of the man born blind from the Synagogue.

Jesus makes a number of statements that would be familiar with his audience;

- He who enters the sheepfold, except by the gate, is a thief or robber.
- He that enters by the gate is the shepherd.
- The watchman opens the gate for him.
- The sheep hear and know his voice.
- He calls out his own sheep and they follow him.
- The sheep do not recognise the voice of a stranger.

At night the sheep from several flocks are gathered in a pen for safety. A shepherd may have sheep in more than one pen. He goes from pen to pen calling his sheep. Those that are his come out and follow him. He then leads them to the best pasture available.

We can put it this way; I am the gate for my sheep. I protect them when they are in and watch over them when they are out. I take care of them. Many have tried to imitate me, but have failed.

In regard to the man born blind Jesus was saying, when he was in your fold you did not take care of him. When he went out you did not watch over him. When you called him, he did not recognise your voice and so he did not follow you. When I called him, he recognised my voice and followed me, because he belonged to me all along. I am the Gate, I will decide who is in and who is out of relationship with God, not you.

It speaks again of that spiritual awakening, that does not save, but prepares a person to respond when they hear the voice of Jesus calling their name. In this he castigates the Jewish leaders for their dereliction of duty, not only in the case of this man, but for the entire House of Israel.

4. I am the Good Shepherd. 10:11-18.

This closely associated with the previous claim. It further turns the screw on the leaders' dereliction of duty.

The Good Shepherd will die for the sheep. The Leaders exploited the people for their own prestige.

The Good Shepherd will have sheep in several pens. This was a real stinging statement. The people who God will call and who will recognise God's voice will not only be Jews, but Gentiles as well.

The Jewish leaders will drive me to my death. But even when I am dead, they will not care for the people. When I rise from the dead, I will call my sheep again and they will follow me. As such he presented himself as the true leader of Israel.

5. I am the Resurrection and the Life. 11:25.

We have covered this exhaustively when we dealt with the Miraculous sign. To step from this life to the next can only be done by totally depending on Jesus. There are no options. I am Lord in this world and the world to come. When Martha spoke of the resurrection on the last day, the day that would inaugurate the Age to Come and the Righteous Kingdom,

Jesus said, that's me, I am that Resurrection. (5:28) He speaks and the dead will rise.

6. I am the way the truth and the life. 14:1-7.

Christianity is not finding a particular path or discovering a special truth, or entering into particular experiences, it is simply staying close to Jesus. In staying close to him we will go the right way, understand what is true, and experience everlasting life.

It's all about destiny. Where are you going? Where are we going?

13:30. Judas *went out and it was night,* he stepped in to the darkness that was his destiny.14:2 I go to prepare a place for you. You are not going into the darkness like Judas.14:31; *come let us go from here.* It's time to step into our destiny. For Jesus it was the cross and then heaven. For the disciples it would be a journey of ministry, but Jesus would be with them on the journey, and wherever the journey took them he would be at the destiny before they got there. I am your way.

The way to his future as risen ascended Lord of Lords, King of Kings, Lamb upon the throne, was through the Cross.

You know the way. You know the place. Between where we are in God to where God is taking you there is probably a cross, but the way is not a dead end, it goes somewhere, we know this because it was not a dead end for Jesus. He went through the cross to the place prepared.

Philip is still perplexed. There will be times when we cannot see the work of the Father. It looks like we are alone. You must still believe in who I am. And if it is so difficult to believe; believe because of what you have seen, heard, and experienced and you will see the hand of God again.

Jesus added, I am not only the way that man comes to the Father, I am the way that the Father comes to man, 'he who has seen me has seen the Father, my revelation of the Father is authentic or true, and he to whom I have given life, the Father has given life.

We can lay down the security of where we are now, for a journey over which we have no control, to come to a place we know not of, but when we get there, we find the Lord is there to receive us.

Let not your hearts be troubled. The future always has the tendency to be scary, nonetheless here. Trust in God; trust in me. As you have believed in the God you have never seen, you can believe in me although shortly you will no longer see me. The subject that is being addressed is the uncertainty of the future and how they will cope with the altered circumstances. This must be born in mind as we consider the next few sentences.

My Father's House. We usually have assumed he meant Heaven. We certainly use the term to describe our eternal abode but the bible does not. In John's Gospel the phrase refers to the temple; but from a Hebrew perspective. The temple was a picture of the final abode of the righteous in the presence of God in the kingdom of the Messiah that was still to come. Isaiah 2:1-5. It is also depicted in Revelation 21:1-4; 22-27; 1Cor 3:16.

The message of the gospel is that this final abode is not altogether confined to the future but is to be experienced in part in the age that was about to dawn upon the world. So amazing was the age to come going to be that it resembled the Father's House in the hearts of believers as they journeyed through a hostile world.

Hebrews 3: 1-6. *'But Christ as son over His own house, whose house we are.'*

Many abiding places; places where you stop for a while and then move on. It can be that you stay in the same place but spiritually you are transformed by the ongoing work of the Holy

Spirit in your lives, or they can be physically moving to another place altogether. They can be short term, long term or permanent. They are different abiding places. They are the outworking of the will of God in your life.

'If it were not so I would have told you' If things were otherwise, I would have told you. Jesus said, *'I go.'* I am moving from one abiding place to another. It is time for me to move on. Don't be troubled about this, I will remain within my Father's House, just in another abiding place. In a little while you will not see me and then you will see me again. As much as I am in my Father's house, you will also be in my Father's house, just in a different abiding place. [31]

'Where I am going, I will prepare a place for you. When you get there, I will be there to receive you. And you know the place and you know the way.'
When Jesus rose from the dead He entered into another abiding place in His Father's house. It is completely different from the abiding place he had been in for last thirty or so years.
The differences are; He could be seen or not seen. He would be present with all who called upon His name wherever they were in space and time. The similarity is that His power and authority remained unchanged.
The way to His future as risen ascended Lord of Lords, King of Kings, lamb upon the throne, was through the Cross.
You know the way. You know the place. Between where we are in God to where God is taking us, we may encounter a 'cross, but that will not be the end. He went through the cross to the place prepared.

The Prepared Place. It is when what you thought to be the light at the end of tunnel is in fact the train coming the other way; or when you realise the rock on which you were standing was in fact sinking sand; or the person whom you were relying

---

[31] **Barnes Commentary on the New Testament.**

on suddenly is no longer there; you will hear him say, *'I have prepared a pace for you.'*

Jesus, the Father and the Holy Spirit will be in the place prepared. It's Father's House, it's **safe, sacred and secret**; the world cannot even see it and Satan has no jurisdiction there.

The prepared place is the next abiding place in our walk with God. There will be peace in our heart; the Holy Spirit will bring to remembrance all that you have learned to equip you for the new place.

Some people know where they are going, some have an idea, many have no idea at all. It's scary, we don't know the way, but we know that Jesus has travelled the road already and he has already arrived at the destination. So, we followed our Lord who dares to call himself 'the way.' It's a laying down of the familiar and comfortable, to these disciples it would not be the same, Jesus would not be there as he had been there, but he will still be there in another dimension. I am preparing the place, and when you step into it you will know that it is designed just for you.

The Final Abiding Place. As we travel our earthly journey within the Father's house, he is preparing us for the place as much as he is preparing the place for us. One day our earthly journey will be over but as we move from this life to the next, we will still be within the Father's house.

Now the teaching moves to describe how this new arrangement will work through the coming of the Holy Spirit.

7. I am the true vine. 15:1-17.

The Vineyard is a symbol of the nation of Israel. Several scriptures allude to this. Most notable is Isaiah 5:1-7. The Vine picture however is not a pleasant one. It always refers to Israel as unproductive deserving only to be pruned or cut out.

- The True Vine is not Israel.
- The Vinedressers are not the Leaders of Israel.
- Israel and its religious system, by now, was producing fruitless branches.
- What the Jewish leaders decided was of value was in fact of no value.

I am the Vine and My Father is the Vinedresser. There will still be pruning and cutting off, but it will according to the criterion of God's grace and Jesus' saving power.

The branch that bears fruit draws its life from the vine. Once again it is totally dependent on the vine. You are the branches. The branch that does not draw its life from the vine withers and dies and is cut down.

15: 7. *'Ask whatever they wish and it will be given you.'* This is not a blank cheque to ask whatever whim of fancy comes to mind. It is qualified in the next verse. God's desire is 'much fruit.' You can ask for as much fruit to be produced in your life as you desire, and it will be granted.

How do we remain in the Vine? By loving God and loving one another as Christ has loved us.

What is the fruit we are to produce?

If the tree produces apples, then it is an apple tree. The life in it is so designed. If the 'tree' is Jesus, then what type of fruit do think will be produced?

Luke 3:9-14. John the Baptizer introduces the concept of a fruit bearing life to the NT. He also tells us what 'fruit' means. Compassionate to the poor; honesty in business; don't take advantage of subordinates; contentment.

Galatians 5:22. Love, joy, peace, patience, kindness, goodness, faithfulness, gentleness, and self-control.

Ephesians 5:9. The fruit of the Light consists in all goodness, righteousness, and truth.

James 3:17. But the wisdom that comes from heaven is first of all pure; then peace-loving, considerate, submissive, full of mercy, and good fruit., impartial and sincere. Peacemakers who sow in peace raise a harvest of righteousness.

In these verses and others in the NT we see that 'fruit' is predominantly to do with a Christlike Character. We can ask for as much of that as we desire. There could some pruning along the way however, in order to produce it.

Who are the ones who are cut off? These are those who do not produce that moral likeness to Jesus. In other words, they are not drawing on the life of the tree.

CHAPTER 7.
SEVEN THINGS
ABOUT THE HOLY SPIRIT

We pick up on the teachings of Jesus, just after the, '*I am going to prepare a place for you,*' comments. The next chapters, 14-17 are largely unique to John. The teaching is to prepare the disciples for the future where Jesus would be physically absent. Jesus begins to explain who the Holy Spirit is, what he will do, and how he is pivotal to their continued witness.

Greater works. 14:12
The 'works' that is the miracles, are the works of God. As they are works that only God can do, it is proof that the Father is with me.
The disciples will do greater works. Not greater in their essential nature. What can be greater than the raising of the dead? But greater in quantity and scope. It will be possible because Jesus is going to the Father. At the Throne of Grace, he can hear the cry of the people of the entire earth, not just those in one location. He will also see the efforts of his servants in the most remote places of the globe, and he will be with them. It will be the same works but they will be multiplied exponentially.

1. He will be like me. 14:16.

Many will be familiar with the Greek word 'Parakletos.' It does not have a singular English equivalent. Different translations have captured the meaning using words all generally meaning, 'one sent alongside to help.'
Advocate. New Living translation.
Comforter. King James Version.
Helper. New American Standard Bible.
Helper, Comforter, Advocate, Intercessor, Counsellor, Strengthener, Standby. Amplified bible.

Let us firstly think of the word 'another.' This of course is stating there is already one of this kind already here. Jesus was speaking of himself. There is another one coming who in his essential nature is the same as me. John, amongst the NT writers, probably tries the most to give us understanding on the mystery of God. He has made it clear that he and the Father are distinct, but of the same essential nature. If the Holy Spirit is of the same nature of Jesus, then by inference they are each of the same nature. This is what eventually became defined as the 'Trinity.' Three persons eternally existing as one.

We shall begin to see that as Jesus was the 'Way, truth, and Life,' so the Holy Spirit will also be the 'Way the Truth and the Life.'
The world, that is the unbeliever, will no longer see me, but you will see me, in the sense you will continue to see my works. Then you will know that not only is the Father in me but you will realise that as the Father is in me, so I am in you. You will talk about me, you will talk to me, you will know my presence and hear my voice, all this will be possible through this 'paraklete' who is coming to dwell in you.

The Spirit of truth. He will present an uncontaminated, uncompromised, and an un-edited presentation of who I am and at the same time who the Father is. You will know when I am speaking because the words you hear will be compatible with the words I have already spoken. That is why we must be familiar with the Word of God, the Bible, because without knowing what has been said, to whom, and in what tone, we will not know if the voice we hear will be the voice of Jesus or not. Jesus will never say anything through the Holy Spirit that is contradictory to what he said in person.

I will not leave you as orphans. We will be a Family; Father, Son, Holy Spirit, and believers as one. The unbeliever will not know this intimacy of relationship.

2. The world will not know him. 14:22-31.

A disciple called Judas asks why this is so. No doubt conjecturing that the best way to take the message to the world is for Jesus to be visible to all.

Jesus had presented himself to all the people, yet it had not resulted in a universal belief. Some had believed and some had refused to believe. It will be the same when Jesus returns to the Father and the disciples take up the mantle of witness. Some will believe and some will not. As only those who believed when he was physically present understood who he was, only those who believe when he has returned to the Father will understand who is. The unbeliever in both cases will be blind as to who he is and will be cut off from the enlightenment of the Holy Spirit. The unbeliever will make their choice on what they see of Jesus in the believer. But the unbeliever will not experience the intimacy of the Holy Spirit until they believe.

If anyone loves me. The Christian experience will be a matter of relationship with Jesus. It will not be in a mere performance of rituals, it will not be in cold submissive obedience, it will not be in observance or applause of the works of God. It will be in a personal relationship with Jesus, sealed by the infilling of the Holy Spirit. We obey him because we love him.

God loves us. God's love for the unbeliever is manifest in that he has provided the way of salvation that they should not perish but have everlasting life.

God's love for the believers is manifest in that he will make his home with them. This 'make our home' reflects further on the 'I will not leave you as orphans. This is one of the 'abiding places' that we have spoken about. The presence of God will be real. The presence of God will not be known at this level among unbelievers.

3. He will teach you all things. 14:26.

The Holy Spirit will come in the name of Jesus. That is, he comes to do the same work with the same authority from the same source. What we believe, what we teach, and what we expect others to believe, is to be based on the teachings of Jesus Christ. We have read that from the beginning he was full of *Grace and Truth.* His own claim ringing in our ears, *'I am the truth.'*

- Jesus revealed how the details of the elaborate ritual of the Mosaic system revealed the meaning of what he was doing. So, we can examine these things and the Spirit will enable us to see Jesus.
- Jesus revealed that the words of the prophets focused on who he was. The Spirit will cause the mystery of God's plan to unfold before our eyes.
- Jesus revealed things that he had heard his Father say in the confines of the Holy Trinity. We can contemplate on these things and the Spirit will make the meanings clear.
- Jesus spoke of things that were to happen after his earthly ministry had ended. The Spirit will enable us to know how and when to apply these truths.

I will leave you with my peace. 14:27. That is, the assurance that although things will be radically different for these men, everything was still very much under control. The 'peace' of Jesus was that the purposes of God would be fulfilled irrespective of what opposition would rise against them. That 'peace' is now our peace. We can walk in the serenity of the Will of God irrespective of what is going on around us.

Rejoice with me. 14:28. Jesus tells the disciples to rejoice at his going away. It is a plea for them to see the bigger picture. No longer were they to only consider themselves, and how things related to them, a handful of men in the land of Israel. But they were to consider what his going away meant to Jesus himself.

- We will never comprehend what it meant to the relationship of the Holy Trinity, for Jesus to take on human form and suffer the humiliation of the cross. But it was apparent that it was a matter of extreme importance to him to take again his rightful place in the heavens. For that they should rejoice.

- His ascending to his Father would mean his absence from them as they had known him, but it would also mean his presence through the Holy Spirit anywhere in the world where someone would call on his name. For that they should rejoice.

- When they lifted their eyes to heaven from now on, in Jesus' Name, and came before the Throne of Grace, there was one on the Throne of God who understood their plight, had felt their pain and walked their rocky road. For that they should rejoice.

- His going away marked the beginning of a new era of God's relationship with mankind which would culminate with his return and the establishment of the Righteous Kingdom which they so longed for. For that they should rejoice.

The prince of this world. This is Satan of course, as he would inspire the actions that were at that moment beginning to unfold. But he has no hold on me. There is no place where he could have gained a foothold in his life, because he was without sin. He can't tempt me to run away; he can't frighten me with his horrors; he can't deceive me with his temptations; and he can't seal me in his grave. What faith! The Holy Spirit will bring these things to your remembrance when you face the fiery trial.

At his point Jesus leaves the place of the Passover meal and walks with his disciples to Gethsemane. The remainder of the conversation takes place along that journey and in Gethsemane itself.

4. He will testify about me. 15: 18-27.

We will pick up the teaching of preparation for the future in 15:18. This first section is linked to 14:30. The 'I am the true vine' statement and its meaning seems to be an interjection in the general theme of their age to come. It is quite possible that this was spoken on the journey to Gethsemane, and once there, the subject returned to the future age.

The Prince of this World, who has no hold on me, will come for you also. This is the world that abides under the wrath of God because it chooses not to believe. That choice is all the foothold that Satan needs to inspire the minds, hearts, and action of the ungodly. But we cannot be kept separate from this world because these are the people to whom the gospel must be preached. Among them there would be a 'Saul of Tarsus,' and he, and others like him, must be given the opportunity to believe.

The hatred of the world is not personal. It is because of our association with Jesus.

It is because when we speak the truth we cut in to the lie of the philosophy of the world.

They hate you because they see you are chosen and consider you as God's favourites. They fail to see that you have gained your privileged status because you believed, and they can also believe.

They hate you; they hate me; they hate the Father. They quickly make the connection that you are representatives of God. God is the one who makes the sinner feel guilty, spiritually impoverished, ashamed and unclean, and so God and his representatives are hated as well. I think everyone knows that the cause of the trauma in our societies today is the moral paucity that prevails, but you point that out at your peril. *'Tell us how much God loves us; how forgiving he is; and about the place of peace he has prepared for us. But don't talk to us about sin!'*

The Holy Spirit will testify. You must testify too. The Holy Spirit will enable us to continue to testify against such opposition. He will not lower the standard, he will not compromise the message, he will not turn a blind eye to sin. He will inspire us as to how and when and to whom to speak, just as Jesus did. 16:1-4. They will put you out of the synagogues, and they will kill in God's Name. By the time John wrote these words they had already come to pass on many occasions.

So that you do not go astray. So great will the opposition be at times that we will be tempted to compromise. But remember it is not us who is testifying, it is the Spirit who has come in his name.

5. The Holy Spirit and the World. 16: 5-16.

'Unless I go away, the Spirit will not come.' This is not saying that somehow The Holy Spirit and Jesus cannot be present at the same time, that somehow, they are swapping places. It is saying that unless Jesus takes the pathway to the cross, the

grave, the heavens, and all that it implies, then the Holy Spirit will not come. He will not come, in this scenario, because there would be no redeemed life which to fill and anoint. But we can give thanks that, in the words of Francis Bottome,

'Let every Christian tongue, proclaim the joyful sound, the Comforter has come!'

John presents to us that the greatest of all sins is the rejection of Jesus Christ as the saviour of the World. What the world perceives as sin changes from time to time. By the noise of current protestations, it seems the view prevails that discrimination, racism, and paedophilia are the most heinous of crimes. They are indeed and so much more, but the greatest of all is the rejection of the gift of salvation. John's position has been consistent; believe and receive eternal life; refuse to believe and perish.

To John it is what Jesus taught and what the Holy Spirit will continue to enforce. Few of the people in the category of 'the world' would agree with that and so that is the source of their hatred against Jesus and his followers. It is illustrated in Mark's account of the Rich Ruler, Mark 10:17-23. As far as the moral law was concerned, he was faultless, but the one thing he lacked, he was not following Jesus. Then Jesus added the words, *'How hard it is to enter the kingdom of God.'*

He will convict, in regard to sin. The basic level of human morality is the conscience. It is to tell us the difference between right and wrong. When I first began to use a machine to write, it was a manual typewriter. The keyboard was the same but they operated a metal lever which pressed the outline of the letter through an ink tape onto the page. When you were coming to the end of the line a bell would ring to say you only had one or two more characters and you would be at the end of the line. Then you had to roll the paper up to the next line. The bell was crucial. The problem was, you set the bell yourself to get small or large margins. That is the weakness of conscience. You can set the bell wherever you want. You can override conscience. The more you override it the less effective it becomes.

The Holy Spirit cannot be manipulated to suit human desires. The bell rings where God has set it. Conversion to Jesus Christ does not begin when we realise we have done bad things, but when we realise we are separated from God because we have never believed that Jesus is the Son of God and the Saviour of the World.

He will convict, in regard to righteousness. *'Because I am going to the Father.'* This righteousness is the righteousness of Jesus himself. The righteousness of Christ was established by his resurrection from the dead. Paul would shortly write, *'if Christ be not risen our preaching and your faith is useless.'* 1 Corinthians 15:12. The resurrection established forever the Father's approval of who Jesus was. If he had been anything less than absolutely righteous, he would never have been raised. Rome condemned him, the Jewish Leadership condemned him, but God vindicated him. At his baptism, on the hill of transfiguration, during the conversation with the Greeks, and finally at the tomb of Joseph; this is the Son of God, the Saviour of the World. It is summed up in Peter's declaration in Acts 2:22-24.

> *Fellow Israelites, listen to this: Jesus of Nazareth was a man accredited by God to you by miracles, wonders and signs, which God did among you through him, as you yourselves know. This man was handed over to you by God's deliberate plan and foreknowledge; and you, with the help of wicked men, put him to death by nailing him to the cross. But God raised him from the dead, freeing him from the agony of death, because it was impossible for death to keep its hold on him.*

147

This is the realisation that as sinners, we were party to the death of the Righteous One. When the old spiritual asks the question, *'Were you there when they crucified my Lord?'* The answer is yes. He died for me. He died instead of me. He died because of me.

There is one thing more than any other which stands a chance of penetrating the hardest heart. It is pure altruistic love. This is when someone does something for another without any thought of personal well-being, reward or safety, just so someone else can be benefitted. That is the message of the Cross and if that doesn't touch the heart, then nothing will. The rejection of the Cross is a rejection of the Holy Spirit. The rejection of the Holy Spirit is the rejection of Christ. The rejection of Christ is the rejection of the Father, and so, such a person remains under the wrath of God awaiting the day of judgement.

He will convict in regard to judgement. To sum this up, the Holy Spirit first shows what is in us. The he shows us who Jesus is. Finally, he shows us what is to come. *'The prince of the world now stands condemned.'* Judgement is another of those unacceptable word in today parlance. You cannot judge me, the sinner squawks. We read that the activity of the cross was Satanically inspired. We see how the Jewish leaders were castigated as *'Children of the Devil'* as they sought to get rid of Jesus. 8:44; and Satan *'entered into '*Judas,13:27. Later the apostles expanded this by describing the Cross as a spiritual conflict between Satan and God. Colossians 2:5; 1Peter 3:16-20. The cross exposed Satan as the source and inspiration behind all evil. Hearts of unbelief tap into that evil and so people commit acts of evil. Acts 2:22-24. They were responsible for their wicked acts. But they committed these acts because of their unbelief. That unbelief tapped into the source of evil. Satan was defeated in the sense that he no longer had access to the hearts of people who believed. Or to put it another way, the believer had gained the power to resist and overcome him. The conviction of the Holy Spirit shows the unbeliever that he has opened his heart to the inspiration of the one who inspired the agony of the cross.

This also introduces the fact that one day all will stand before Jesus and be judged as to why they chose unbelief over belief.

To bring about true conviction, the Holy Spirit reaches deep into the heart of a man and shows the sin that is there, he shows the righteousness of Christ and the fact that everyone will be responsible for the choices they make. Then that person is free to make a choice to belief or not to believe.

6. The Holy Spirit and the Believer. 16:12-16.

He will tell us things when we need to hear them. As the disciples went out into the world, they found circumstances they had never dreamed of. They faced people with complex problems and convoluted circumstances, that Jesus realised that there was no one-sentence answer or instruction to guide them. They would have to deal with the situations as they found them. But how were they going to make the right decisions?

Matthew 10:17-20. The Holy Spirit will aid you in what you have to say. This does not mean that we do not need to study God's Word, or prepare when we present the gospel. Not at all. But when you are caught up in the unpredictability of the moment and when the circumstances are controlled by nefarious characters, then *'I will give you what to say.'*

As the believer speaks, the Holy Spirit can take his words and turn them into a specific message to one person in the audience. The speaker did not know he was addressing that person, but the Spirit did, and the person did. Such things can be of deep spiritual significance to those involved. As time went by, they would become aware of things to day we call

the 'gifts of the spirit.' Paul wrote about it in 1 Corinthians 12:
1-11. Paul mentions message gifts, prophecy, tongues and
interpretation of tongues; he mentions gifts of power, faith,
miracles and healings; and he mentions gifts of insight,
wisdom, knowledge, and discernment of spirits. But the
emphasis he points out, above all is, *'these are all the work of
the one and the same Spirit and he gives them to each one
just as he determines.'* In other words, they become evident
whenever the Spirit determines they are necessary.

He will guide us. The Spirit of truth will guide us into all truth.
That does not mean that we make it up as we go along and
the Holy Spirit gives it approval, or even, may I say, the Holy
Spirit makes it up as we go along. The truth exists. It is the
revelation of God and God's plan of world redemption. It was
devised before the foundation of the world. Ephesians 1:3-10;
Colossians 1: 25-27. The Spirit leads us into that which is
already complete.
Jesus is the one who was there at the beginning. He was God.
He was the Word. He formed everything. He is the truth. The
guiding of thew Holy Spirit leads us to know more about
Jesus.

He will not speak of himself. The Holy Spirit is the most
mysterious of the persons of the trinity. The word 'Spirit'
makes it so. Although he is a co-equal person with the Father
and the Son, he is presented in a much more obscured way.
He never speaks himself as to be heard, he always inspires
the voice of others. He never says 'I am' or anything in
reference to himself, he only ever says, Jesus is the 'I am.' He
does not control us as a puppet master, but gently whispers,
this way not that. And when a job is finished, you have a
preacher who has preached, people who are changed, you
have a miracle, or Divine Wisdom, but he is nowhere to be
seen. That is the Holy Spirit. There were occasions when
Jesus had performed a miracle or said something pertinent,

there was a reaction to make him king. As a result, he had to retreat and hide from the situation to see that it didn't happen. The Glory of the moment would go to the Father. So, it is with the Spirit. He remains hidden so the glory goes to Jesus.

He will speak what he hears. Jesus himself made this claim many times. 7:16 etc.,
He is always repeating what he hears in conversations within the Godhead. It is like a radio signal. Its beaming out the message all the time. But you can't hear it unless you tune in. He never stops. He requires mean and women filled with the Holy Spirit to tune in to his wavelength.

He takes what is mine. This is one of the indispensable checks of the supernatural. People can take advantage of the mysterious nature of the Holy Spirit in order to deceive. Anyone can stand up and say the Holy Spirit told me to say this or that with some conviction, How do we then know if it is true or not? If, when all is said, the result of the occasion illuminates anyone but Jesus, a healer, a preacher, a leader, then you can lay it aside as not being of the Holy Spirit. If someone says something that would contradict the nature of the Jesus we know from scriptures, you can lay it down. The Spirit has not spoken. If a person claims revelations of the past, present or future, by the Spirit, which are intriguing, captivating, even mesmerising, but revealing nothing about Jesus, then leave them alone.
The Holy Spirt takes from what belongs to Jesus, and makes it known to us.

He will tell you what is to come.
I don't think this means a detailed 'diary' of the future. Rather a 'next few steps' of the future as in Acts 20:22-24; a general scenario of the last days as in 1Timothy 4:1-4; and the return of the Lord as in 1 Thessalonians 4:13-18.

The book of Revelation is of course the most extensive and panoramic prophetic document in the NT. And John says that he wrote it as a result of 'being in the Spirit.' But to say it is a detailed outline of the ages until Christ's return is stretching the truth somewhat.

He will enable you to see something of the consequences of a decision or action, either for you or for someone else, so you can decide whether to press on or change course.

He will bring glory to me.

'Glory' means, prestige, fame, renown, honour, and pre-eminence. The work of the Holy Spirit is to Glorify Jesus. The individual Christian or the gathered Community should, as a result of being filled with the Spirit, exude Christlikeness.

7. The Holy Spirit will bring times of Great Joy. 16:16-33.

We must bear in mind that when we read these verses, they are plain enough to us, because we read them with hindsight. But to the disciples the things that are clear to us were a total mystery to them. His departure and re-appearance after 'a little while,' to us, is his burial and resurrection. But death, burial and resurrection were not in the framework of their thinking.

Speaking 'figuratively' could be understood as parables or proverbs. [32] Speaking in parables had a specific purpose. It was to make a statement that was somewhat obscured. The hearer would know something significant had been said but the meaning of it would only become clear on reflection and questioning. This is explained in Matthew 13:10-17. The parable would be like a bait to further understanding. Only those who reflected and questioned would understand. That response would show whose heart had been awakened to

---

[32] **Barnes' Notes on the Bible.**

discover truth. Those who were satisfied with the story without concern for its meaning, would be the one's *'ever hearing but not understanding, ever seeing but never perceiving.*

This section of text shows us that the disciples had passed that test and they were hungry nor only for the information at face value, but for its meaning and implications as well.

A huge amount of our preaching and teaching is still done through parables and figures of speech. It is because we are trying to convey spiritual things that have no precedence in a carnal world. We paint the word picture, apply it and leave it to the Holy Spirit to turn it into the experience of someone's life. That moment when the word picture becomes a life-changing experience, is that 'awakening' of the human spirit to Divine Revelation.

'Now you are speaking clearly,' shows us that was what was happening to the disciples. To put it in modern parlance, 'Now we get it!'

What had happened was that they realised that Jesus had accurately read their thoughts without them being spoken and answered their questions without them being asked. This is indicative of how it will be when the Holy Spirit comes. *'In that day,'*

The parable in question is the illustration of childbirth. 16: 19-22. The meaning is that they would pass through a times of grief and pain, but that would be turned into joy and celebration which would never fade away. Once again, we readily understand the meaning, but it was not so easy for them. Their understanding of his going away, was that he was going to the Father for a while and would return to them, not that he was going by the way of a cross and a grave.

It was also a picture of how their ministry would be when the Spirit came. There would be times of sorrow and times of joy. What would be achieved through the Holy Spirit will eclipse any of the pain endured in order to see it happen.

In the day of the Holy Spirit, they will not have need to ask for things to be explained. The word 'ask' here, is better understood as 'inquired.' The Holy Spirit will make things plain to them. They will be able to explain things to others. [33]

Then we have 'ask' as in request. In the day of the Holy Spirit, you may ask the Father in my name. To pray 'in his name' is more than asking for a list of things that we feel will be beneficial to us or others and adding the suffix, 'in your name, amen.' Such a suffix does not sanctify the prayer and guarantee the answer. To ask in his name is to ask for something, that had Jesus been present, it would have been the type of thing he would have readily done. It is a request, that if granted, would bring renown to his name in the same way as it was when he was still present on earth. In this context, the believer can ask anything.

You joy will be fulfilled.

This comes from 15:11. *'I have told you this that my joy may be in you and that your joy may be full.'* Jesus was saying that his joy would be when Father, Son, Spirit and believer are in loving communion together. His joy would also be the source of our joy. Our joy would be the experience of the presence of God in our lives as a constant companion, in the night of weeping and the morning of joy. In the closing verses of this section Jesus says, *'you will be scattered.'* Again, this is directly to do with the crucifixion, but it was also indicative of their future. There would be times when they would be alone. No one else to comfort or care for them. Yet they would not be alone, as he would not be alone, because the Holy Spirit would be in them wherever they were compelled to go.

Their joy would be full when they presented the Gospel to the nations, and people also believed who had not seen or heard what they had. But they would believe because of their faithful witness. Ephesians 1:15-18.

---

[33] **Barnes' Notes on the Bible**

This would be the essence of the joy of the Age of the Holy Spirit.

In the world they would have trouble, but in their relationship with Jesus they would have peace. This reflects the dichotomy of the Christian life. As the NT unfolds, we find it stated in different ways; the earthly and heavenly; the temporal and the eternal; the carnal and the spiritual; the weak and the strong; the old nature and the new nature. The world, its structures, governments, civilisations, and ambitions, would never be in harmony with the spirit-filled believer. The opposition would vary from place to place and circumstance to circumstance, but do not be deceived, you will have trouble. And it will continue as such until Jesus returns again with the brightness of his coming, and established the Righteous Kingdom on earth. 2 Thessalonians 1:3-10.

CHAPTER 8.
SEVEN HIGHLIGHTS
FROM THE PRAYER

This prayer is offered by our Lord most probably on the way to Gethsemane. 18:1. We cannot imagine that such a prayer as this would have been offered while Jesus was walking along. Much more likely they had stopped at some place along the way. It is not the prayer at the time of the arrest, *'Father not my will.'* That prayer comes after this one. It is called either the Farewell Prayer or the High priestly Prayer. The prayer naturally falls into three sections, a prayer for himself, a prayer for the disciples, and a prayer for those who would believe through their testimony.

As in all the sections of the Gospel seven steps can be seen in this chapter.

1. That they may know you. 17:1-5.

'Raising his eyes to heaven,' as the NASB renders it, encompasses us in the solemnity of the moment. On the one hand we are eavesdropping on a conversation between two persons of the Trinity, and one the other a man calling upon his God. We will never understand the mystery of godliness. It is the way it is and we are advised just to accept it.

Glorify your Son. This is the 'hour,' or the specific time we have spoken about from before the world began. The glory of God had been swallowed up into humanity, and shortly that humanity would be swallowed up in mortality, but even that mortality would be swallowed up in ignominy. To Glorify the Son clothed in his rightful Deity, was no problem; he was the image of the invisible God. To Glorify Jesus as the sinless man was also without difficulty. But to Glorify him as a lifeless corpse and the ignominy of false accusations abuse and shame was another thing. 'Father, from the opprobrium of Joseph's tomb will you restore the Glory I had with you before the world began.'

When people in the age to come look upon the cross they will come to know the God who acted vicariously; compassionately; decisively and effectively to take away the sin of the world and they will Glorify your name.

Knowing God and Jesus Christ who you sent is Eternal Life. Knowing God is not being able to explain the mystery of the trinity, or be able to expound the meanings of his many names and titles, knowing God is to feel the heartbeat of the God who acted at calvary.

2. Those you have given me. 17:6-10

Granted him authority. Jesus was appointed to be the saviour of all, and paid the price for the sin of all the world, knowing full well that only some would believe, and of those who initially believed one would fall away. But for those who believed he granted eternal life. They already knew the Father as the Almighty God; the Eternal God; the Covenant God; and the Creator God. But now they knew him as the Saving God; the Healing God; the Restoring God; the Delivering God, and the Loving God. The work with them was complete, they believed. They have seen the miracles, they heard the conversations, they have witnessed the arguments, they have heard the claims, and at each stage, they believed. They have believed that I came from the Father and will return to the Father, therefore they have received eternal life that they may have everlasting communion with us.

We have seen as we have travelled with John in this remarkable odyssey that Jesus did not make the status of belief an easy thing. He always searched for what was in the heart of man. He immediately embraced Nathaniel as a man of a pure heart. 1: 47. Yet he avoided the observers in Jerusalem because he knew they were there to be entertained, not to believe. 2:24. Jesus scattered the multitude in chapter six because they would follow, but not believe. 6:64-66. To address your audience as 'children of the devil,' was not the best way to win over a crowd. 8:44. But he was not trying to win over a crowd, he was searching for those whom the Father had prepared.

We see that salvation is not the choice of God without the co-operation of man. It is not the choice of man without the co-operation of God. It is a blend of God's choice and man's choice. We can say no more because it is lost in the mystery of sovereign grace, but of this we can be assured, no one comes to Jesus unless the Father draws him.6:44. '*I am praying, not for the world, but for those you have given me.*' We have seen that God's love for the unbelieving world consists of providing a way of salvation that they may believe. But his love for those who have crossed the threshold of belief is on a different level. With them he establishes an ongoing relationship whereby, in all circumstances they will be conscious of his presence.

3. Protect them. 17:11-12.

The disciples were to remain in the world for their lifetime. They had been in the world before Jesus came. The difference now was, because of their encounter with the Saviour, they were no longer of this world. This was an existential crisis. They no longer belonged to their familiar surroundings. Their relationship with Galilee; Israel; Judaism;

the Temple; and even to some extent, their families, was changed forever. They were now citizens of a new kingdom. There was no protection from the Jewish leaders or from the Roman leaders. They belonged to a Kingdom that did not have diplomatic relations with the kingdoms of the world. Some would ignore them; some would tolerate them; and others would accommodate them, but none would protect them.

That is why Jesus has emphasised their inter-dependence, *'Love one another.'* On earth, when all was said and done, they would only have each other.

The believer needs protection from those who would seek to harm to them. But more importantly the believer needs protection from the Evil One.

The loss of Judas is the disturbing factor.

The danger was they could be distracted from the mission by other agenda's, (Acts 1:6) discouraged by terrifying opposition (Acts 8:1-3), or compromised by returning to familiar ground. (Galatians 3:1-5)

The power of your Name- the name you gave me.

'The name of the Lord is a strong tower, the righteous run into to it and they are safe.' Proverbs 18:10.

The Name he was given is the name 'Yehoshua' in Hebrew. Matthew 1:21.

'Yahweh saves.' During the inter-testament period, the Hebrew form was shortened to 'Yeshua,' but the meaning remained the same. From the Hebrew, through Greek and into Latin, the name became 'Iesus.' Latin had both a consonant and a vowel 'i.' During the 11th century Latin scribes devised the letter 'J' to become the consonant. By the 15th century, when the Bible was first translated in to English it would have been rendered 'Jesus.' And that is what has remained ever since.

There is nothing magical in the name or the pronunciation. The point that is being made is that it is the person who holds the name that has the power and authority. Acts 3: 6; 4:10-12.

The power was operative through Jesus because he was one with the Father. The power would be operative with the disciples as they were one with Christ.

4. The full measure of my joy. 17:13-15

Jesus was intimating that he was saying these things while he was still in the world, but the comments concerned the time when he will have returned to the Father.

My joy. The joy that the mission is accomplished. The joy the Holy Spirit is given.

The joy that Satan is defeated. The joy that the gospel will be offered to the entire world. The joy that millions will be saved. Hebrews 12:2.

That they may have the full measure of my joy within them.

A satisfying joy. The joy that Jesus experienced was, in the first place, a joy of satisfaction. It is comparable with the similar human emotion of accomplishment, experienced when a job has been well done. He could look back over the last three to four years and say with satisfaction, 'I wouldn't have done anything differently.' Grant this joy to these men, and indeed to all believers in my name. looking back over many years of ministry I cannot say I wouldn't have done anything different, but I do feel a sense of deep satisfaction that there are large numbers of people who have come to faith and passed it on to others, in spite of my shortcomings. Grant them the joy that when they join me at the Father's side they can look back and say they fulfilled their part in the great commission.

A victorious joy. Jesus' joy was evidenced when he confronted Satan and overcame him. The plans and schemes of the Evil One did not hinder, thwart, or cancel the will of God. He was filled with joy when Satan retreated from the scene of the temptations; when the man of Gadara was in his right mind; when the woman with curved spine stood up straight;

and so many more incidents, including the morning the angels rolled away the stone of Joseph's tomb. His prayer was that his disciples would know this experience of joy as they confronted the evil one on their journey of faith.

A joy of fellowship. Jesus was overcome with joy when in fellowship with the Father. He anticipated the day when 'normal relationship' would be restored without the encumbrance and complication of human form.

His prayer was that the disciples would come to appreciate the presence of the Father and the joy of belonging to his family. The isolation from the world, friends and family, and the abandonment of ambitions and dreams, would be compensated by the joy of knowing they belonged to the Father.

A joy of approval. Jesus is full of joy when the Father voiced his approval. *'This is my Son on whom my favour rests.'* Humanly speaking it is a source of great joy to be told by one superior to ourselves that the job was of the highest standard. It was important to know not only a sense of self satisfaction, but to know the Father was satisfied as well. His prayer was that they would hear loud and clear the voice of the Father as he had done, *'Well done my good and faithful servant, come and share your masters' happiness.'* Matthew 25:21-23.

Jesus was praying these things because he knew that these essential emotional supports would not be forthcoming from the world. They were no longer of the world and would receive no more joy from the world. He knew that in order for them to be emotionally balanced they needed to share in his joy.

5. Sanctify them. 17: 15-19

Jesus prayed that they are not taken out of the world but that they are protected in the world. The world will never be without a witness to who Jesus is. There will be a witness to the truth right up until the day Jesus returns to establish his Righteous Kingdom. Matthew 28:20.

I sanctify myself that they too may be sanctified. 'Sanctify' is to be thought of as a word meaning separation. It comprises of the idea that inspiration, ambition and social conduct. It means to be anchored in one's relationship with the Father, and not in any political, cultural, or demographic model, in favour at any particular time. The well from which the water of sanctification is drawn is to be the Word of Truth. This leads us to understand that at the heart of sanctification lies a set of absolutes. **The** Truth; **the** God; **the** Right and **the** Wrong, amongst others. Today, in the western world, as in the first century, we are free to believe in anything and conduct our lives as we wish. Anything, that is, except declare something to be absolutely true. Those who believe have set out on the journey of sanctification and subsequently are constrained by the characteristics of God himself. It is a process of becoming *one as we are one.'* 'The truth' does not imply a total agreement of every nuance of doctrine. The Truth is essentially the truth about Jesus, who he was, what he said and what he did.

Jesus attended a wedding, celebrations, social occasions, and religious festivals. He spoke the common language and wore the same clothes as everyone else. Yet the source of his morality, spirituality, and ethical standards was not from the prevailing authorities of the day, but from the heart of the Father. He did not say what the Leaders wanted him to say, but what he had heard his Father say. He did not do what they tried to get him to do, but he did what he saw his Father do. As with Jesus, sanctification will always make the believer different. But there will be times when sanctification arouses such rage in the unbeliever that there is persecution.

6. Those who will yet believe on me. 17:20-22

This is the third section of the prayer and follows a distinctive pattern for prayer; oneself; those near; those afar. Jesus looks beyond the cross and sees into a day to come when these men will take the gospel as he had brought the gospel. Their preaching would be as effective as his own, and so the whole thing would be reciprocated down the ages. Men and women being saved, healed, delivered, transformed by the preaching of the gospel.

Several of the world's religions propagate the idea that you are born into that religion and that is the way it is until you die. It is passed on generationally. One generation teaches the next.

Christianity was designed to be different. However sadly, there are large sections of Christianity that rely more on the generational idea than personal conversion. To be born of Christian parents is an advantage, or it should be. But to become a Christian it requires the person to have an individual encounter with Jesus and to be personally filled with the Holy Spirt. Jesus did not count the religious people around him as his followers, even though they were all Jews. His followers were those the Father had drawn to him, and personally decided to follow him.

Generational religion tends to become very legalistic. The customs and traditions are religiously transmitted down the generations and are re-enacted with precision, but there is no personal dynamic encounter with any divine being the religion focuses on. It is simply performing the rituals.

Christianity is less concerned with specific rituals, than it is with ensuring a person has a personal encounter with Jesus. As a result, Christianity always seems to be re-inventing itself. What in fact is happening I believe, is a continual returning to the source, as people discover Jesus and the Holy Spirit afresh. This has the effect of checking legalism and traditionalism, so the church does not return to a system of doing the traditional thing, without understanding why.

On the surface it looks as if Christianity has become increasingly fragmented. Many churches have impacting names that somehow reflect their heartbeat or link them to their community. This can give the impression of separation from the next church, but actually it has created a greater unity. We now find church communities working in increasing cohesion irrespective of their ecclesiastical background. The unity has come about because the person of Jesus has become the focus rather than particular doctrinal emphasis.

7. That they may be brought to complete unity. 22: 23-26.

This brings us the final part of the prayer, *'that they may be one.'* The unity of the Christian community is to be found in the person of Jesus. John wrote these things that we may believe in Jesus. Everything is there to bring us back to the saviour. The complete unity that Jesus prayed for was not that we would all become Anglicans, Baptists or Pentecostals. It was not, that whichever church you went into, anywhere in the world, they would be doing the same thing in the same way. It was that every believer would have a personal encounter with Jesus, and be filled with the Holy Spirit. The people for whom Jesus was praying were still, *'the one's you have given me.'* Those whose spirit has been awakened to who Jesus is.

That they may be with me where I am. Jesus is praying that all who believe will be found worthy of dwelling in the Most Holy presence of the Ever-living God.

That they may behold my glory. The glory or renown of Jesus can mean three things. The glory he had with the Father before the world began, his eternal place in the Godhead. The glory he received as the God-man, shown in his sinless life.

The glory he received as the resurrected saviour, the conqueror of Satan sin and death. It was the desire of Jesus that those who believed would behold him in all his fulness, not only as he was revealed in human form. We catch a glimpse of what this may mean when we look at the words of John's Revelation;

And they sang a new song, saying:

"You are worthy to take the scroll and to open its seals,
because you were slain, and with your blood you purchased
for God
persons from every tribe and language and people and
nation.
You have made them to be a kingdom and priests to serve
our God,
and they will reign on the earth."
Then I looked and heard the voice of many angels,
numbering thousands
upon thousands, and ten thousand times ten thousand.
They encircled the throne and the living creatures and the
elders.
In a loud voice they were saying:
"Worthy is the Lamb, who was slain,
to receive power and wealth and wisdom and strength
and honour and glory and praise!"
Then I heard every creature in heaven and on earth
and under the earth and on the sea, and all that is in them,
saying:
"To him who sits on the throne and to the Lamb
be praise and honour and glory and power,
for ever and ever!" The four living creatures said, "Amen,"
and the elders fell down and worshiped.
Revelation 5:6-14. NIV.

CHAPTER 9.
SEVEN STEPS
TO
JOSEPH'S TOMB.

If the confession of Thomas, *'My Lord and my God,'* is the utmost expression of belief then these verses that cover the passion of Jesus culminate in the utmost expression of unbelief, *'crucify him.'* With these thoughts uppermost in his mind, John omits much detail that is contained in the other gospels. We will refer to some things to help us better understand the text in front of us.

1. The Final Miracle. 18: 1-11

John tells us of the incident when Peter cut off the servant's ear but he does not tell us of the miraculous healing of the wound. For that detail we are indebted to Luke 22:51.

Jesus kept an appointment with Judas.

Jesus was in no doubt as to what was going to happen at Gethsemane. The appearance of Judas was no surprise at all. He knew this was the moment he would be handed over into the hands of those who would put him to death. He kept the appointment, although he had nothing to do with the arrangement, because he had determined to do the will of God. He was determined to do what was required to break the curse of Adam that held the human race in bondage and forbade a renewed relationship with God. We reflect on the times John said words to the effect, 'He hid from them, they tried to take him but could not.'

Satan had entered into Judas.13:27. In the accounts of the temptation of Jesus, Satan attempted to divert Jesus from his mission and save his own life. When Peter said that he would never let Jesus die, 'Satan' was a word Jesus used for Peter, not Judas! Peter was the obstructor not Judas. Matthew 16:23.

What had happened? The plan of Satan had changed from trying to divert him from his destiny to ensuring his destiny was a painful and torturous as possible, so he would turn from it. Satan took hold of the weaknesses of Judas' character, and Judas did not resist. It seems, as we have said, along with others, his mind was pre-occupied with restoring the earthly kingdom and his position in it.

He loved possessions, he embezzled the funds; he loved pre-eminence, he got the seat next to Jesus at the last supper; he loved power, he was accepted in the circles of the Romans, Pharisees and the High Priest. 18:3.

Yet the role of the betrayer was prophesied many times in the OT. Psalm 41:9; Isaiah 53:3; Zechariah 13:7; and the words of Jesus, Matthew 26:24.

Acts 2:22-24. God handed him over.

The atoning death of Jesus was God's idea for world redemption as pictured in the account of Abraham and Isaac. Genesis 22:1-19.

Did Judas have any choice in the matter? He certainly did! God placed his Son to a sinful world, some believed, some took him and connived to slay him because of their unbelief. Both believer and unbeliever stood before Jesus and made a choice.

We stand in the same place. We believe or refuse to believe. We are warned from this incident to develop a 'pure heart.' Only the pure in heart will see God. Areas of our heart that are not sanctified by the Holy Spirit are potential footholds for

Satan. 13:10. In times of crisis and pressure, these areas of our heart can be influenced to make catastrophic decisions.

Jesus gave one more display of who he actually was.
It doesn't exactly say what happened, but describes its effect. Jesus once again uses the divine name, 'I am.' In the use of that name there was a manifestation of the Divine Presence, so much so, those that had come to arrest him were thrown down to the ground, including Judas. He was saying, you must do what you have to do, but you must also know exactly who you are dealing with. They were not taking him; he was giving himself over to them. They were no longer ignorant of what they were doing. They were laying their hands on the Son of God.

Jesus stood in the place of his disciples.
'Let these men go.' They are not the atoning sacrifice, I am. This is one of the truths of the Cross. Jesus died for me. He suffered in my place. The just for the unjust. He stood in my stead. And so, it is declared before sinful men and Satan that inspired them. He says the same to each believer today, *'Let these men go.'*
1 Peter 2: 21-25.

> *'To this you were called, because Christ suffered for you, leaving you an example, that you should follow in his steps He committed no sin and no deceit was found in his mouth. When they hurled their insults at him, he did not retaliate; when he suffered, he made no threats. Instead, he entrusted himself to him who judges justly He himself bore our sins in his body on the cross, so that we might die to sins and live for righteousness; by his wounds you have been healed.'*

Peter drew his sword and cut off the ear of a man called Malchus.

Luke 22:35-38 helps us understand the significance of this. Jesus refers them back to the time when he first commissioned them. He told them to take no provisions. He then asked them if they lacked anything. They said no. Now he says something completely different. Take a purse, a bag and buy a sword. Peter replied that they had two swords and Jesus said, *'that is enough'*.

He was saying, if you already have a bag and purse then keep it. The disciples had obviously moved from their earlier position of faith and had acquired these things. They also had swords. They were ready for the battle to redeem Israel. Jesus' words implied, if you haven't got a sword, in this state of mind, you may as well get one. You are preparing for something that is not going to happen. Why did he say this? So that he could fulfil the scriptures where it said, *'he was numbered with the transgressors.' Isaiah 53:12; Luke 22:37.*

When the soldiers and Jewish officials found Jesus there must be sufficient evidence to convince them they were indeed about to launch a rebellion. We are not going to do this, but it must look as if we are so that I can be arrested as a criminal. Jesus said the two swords were enough, not to start a war, but to achieve that purpose. Jesus was without sin. There was nothing in his life that could associate him the 'transgressors,' so something had to be fabricated. Matthew 26:55. They did not arrest Jesus in the temple courts because they saw no evidence of criminality. But in Gethsemane they did.

The sword was not to be used in anger but was there with the bags and purses to incriminate Jesus.

Peter had not grasped this, and who can blame him? So, he puts his sword to use. Doubtless he did not aim to cut off an ear, he had a more fatal blow in mind. *'Put the sword away.'* This is not the kingdom I have come to establish. If there is any protection needed, I can ask my Father to send angels. But I must drink this cup. They that draw the sword will die by the sword. Jesus was now a sacrifice in the hands of God. They were now constrained by the predictions of scripture.

So, Jesus performed the final miracle of his earthly ministry. He restored the man's ear. This man would have no charge to lay against Peter or Jesus, there was no evidence. His ear was whole. Never again would it be necessary to use a weapon in the cause of the Gospel. A sword would have its place in the matters of justice and freedom, but not to fulfil the plan of world redemption. Those first disciples, and ourselves, need to take heed of the situation as it was at the beginning. No purse, no bag, no need. God supplied it all. When it comes to the Gospel the Holy Spirit will be all the power and force that is needed.

I wonder what happened to Malchus?

2. The Religious Trials. 18:12-27.

In piecing together the accounts in all the gospels we can determine that Jesus faced six inquisitions or trials, 3 religious and 3 civil.

The religious trials were before Annas, the previous High Priest, Caiaphas the current High Priest, and the Sanhedrin, or Jewish Council of State.

The High Priesthood was corrupt. Annas was the patriarch and the power behind the throne. His sons had all taken turns at being the High Priest and it had now passed to his son-in-law.

John tells us that they were interested in his disciples and what he had taught.18:9.

Luke tells us that the bone of contention was that he claimed to be the Son of God. Luke 22:70,71.

Mark tells us they assembled false evidence and settled on the accusation he threatened to destroy the temple and build another one himself.

It sums up under the heading. Blasphemy. He is making himself equal with God. There has been much theological debate on the matter. Did Jesus claim to be God? Some Christian scholars have denied it. Sceptics have said it was an invention of the church at a later date. In deciding exactly what Jesus said and what he meant by it, it can be helpful to not only examine the words of Jesus, but to also examine what the people believed they heard. Without doubt, whatever obscurities there may be in translation, these people were convinced that he said, and he meant to say, he was equal with God.

Guilty as charged.

The procedure began in haste.

We are told the pressure was to get the job done before the Sabbath. They had about 18 hours. We can deduce that the haste was so that the supporters of Jesus would not get to know what was going on until it was too late.

Jesus immediately calls the sham nature of the trial.

Why are you asking me what I taught, you were all there? We discussed it over and over. Why are we going over it all again? By this response Jesus was also saying, you have already reached your verdict so whatever I say to you now will make no difference. He was struck for exposing the unscrupulous method of the High priest.

He is taken on to Caiaphas and the Sanhedrin.

The method is the same, to try and get Jesus to say some self-incriminating statement, but he remains silent.

Then he is asked if he is the Christ, the Son of God.' Matthew 26:63-66. His reply is remarkable. In English we do not feel the potency or grasp the gravitas of his words. His reply is in a typical rabbinical manner. He takes two scriptures linked together by the same theme and takes extracts from each scripture to form his reply. This method is called, 'D'rash.' The rules are; each separate verse must have a common meaning in the 'face value' of the text. When the extracts are put together it cannot contradict the 'face value' meaning only enhance it.

Jesus here quotes from Daniel 7:13. The Son of Man is indisputably recognised as the Messianic figure.

He then quotes from Psalm 110:1-2. Sitting at the right hand of the Mighty One. This is also clearly understood as Messianic.

Finally, he returns to Daniel 7:13 and employs the phrase, 'the clouds of heaven. By the use of these terms linked together in this way Jesus was saying that he is the Messiah of Hebrew Scripture; he is the Messiah standing before them; and he is the Messiah to come at the end of days.

Furthermore, it was another principle of rabbinical interpretation that to quote a fragment of a text was to quote the whole context where it came from. When we read the text around these verses, we can see that there is no doubt as to his meaning. The Sanhedrin also had no doubt.

The contrast with Peter.

John only gives a brief reference to Peter's denial. The other gospels give more detail. We shall stay with John intended purpose. While Jesus was making it absolutely clear who he was, Peter denied three times. Matthew tells us he firstly said, 'he didn't know what they were talking about;' then he said, he didn't know the man;' and then he uttered abuse. Now we must ask, to whom was the abuse directed? Matthew and Mark tell us that he brought the curses on himself. If you will pardon the crudity, he said something like, *'I'll be damned if I ever knew him.'*

And there we have the example for everyone, throughout history, who has been brought before a court of Godless men for their faith in Christ, tell it as it is.

The tearing of the garments.
Matthew and Mark tell us that the religious trials are concluded with the pronunciation of blasphemy and the Priest tearing his garments. Note that this act was a solemn part of the procedure. Caiaphas, corrupt as he was, nevertheless had the responsibility of bearing the sins of the nation before God so the people would not be destroyed, just as Aaron, the first High Priest did. Leviticus 16:15-17. His act of tearing his garment was to acknowledge he had heard, what he believed to be a heinous sin, and he was absorbing the responsibility for that sin into his person as the High Priest so that he could go before the Lord and make the appropriate sacrifices, so that it could be forgiven and the people would not perish. But his act was futile. Not only had Jesus asserted that he was indeed the Messiah and Saviour of the world, but it would shortly be asserted that he was the High Priest of a New Order. Matthew and Mark give us the final detail of the religious implications of the trial of Jesus. God tore his own garment when Jesus died. Matthew 27:51; Mark 15:38. The veil of the temple was made in exactly the same way as the High Priests robes, just a lot bigger. God was saying that he himself would take responsibility for the sin of man on the basis of Jesus' death. The writer of the book of Hebrews takes this imagery further. Hebrews 4:14-5:10.
As a result of the religious trial Jesus asserts himself as the true Messiah of Israel and the saviour of the world, and in addition he is revealed as the true High Priest that takes away the sin of the world.

3. The Civil trial. 18:28-19:16.

The 3 Civil trials were before Herod and twice before Pilate.

The matter that was put to Herod and Pilate was that Jesus was preparing a rebellion to overthrow the Roman occupation.

As far as Herod was concerned, he was the King of the Jews, and the Romans were happy with that situation.

Herod.

John tells us nothing about the trial with Herod but Luke does. Luke 23:8-13. It seems Herod treated is a bit of a joke. His questions were unanswered. This trial concluded with Herod and his soldiers mocking Jesus by dressing him as a king and abusing him. He was taunting Jesus by saying as it were, if you want to be king you have to get past me first, and how do you propose to do that? Herod probably considered Jesus insane, but he did not find him guilty of a crime. Luke 23:15.

Pilate.

They would not enter Pilate's court because it would make them 'unclean' to eat the Passover. 18:28. How strange that they were so concerned about their religious ritual while at the same time crucifying the Son of God. How futile are religious rituals when they are performed without a personal encounter with the Saviour. Even today, people will go to war over their religious rituals at the drop of a hat but they will not believe in the Saviour.

Pilate's first question is, *'Are you the King of the Jews?'* To which Jesus replied, *'Is that your own idea or did others talk to you about me?'*

The crucial word is 'King.' To unscramble the words, it would seem that Jesus is saying, 'How do you use the word King? Is it as the Jewish Leaders use it, that I am conducting a rebellion, or do you understand it as I do, that I have come to establish a spiritual kingdom?

Pilate's answer is basically, 'I have no idea.' You been handed over to me, what have you done?

The key is 18:36,37. *My kingdom is not of this world. If it were, my servants would fight to prevent my arrest by the Jews. But now my kingdom is from another place…you are right in saying I am a king. In fact, for this reason I was born, and for this I came into the world, to testify to the truth. Everyone on the side of truth listens to me.*

Throughout the centuries there have been many attempts to merge the gospel of Jesus Christ with human governments. The bishops of Rome attempted this for about 1000 years, until the reformation. This achieved little in the way of spiritual or moral behaviour and was mainly a political thing to dominate as much of mankind as possible and call it 'The Christian Kingdom' or Christendom.

The golden dawn of the reformation, bought with the blood of thousands of Godly men and women, quickly passed when the now independent Christian groups tried to do the same things, merge the nation state with Christianity. In England in the 17th century, Cromwell's protectorate, tried it and failed, as did the dissenters who sailed to America and later to found colonies in other parts of the world the world.

The civil trial of Jesus reveals to us the truth, the Kingdom of God cannot be merged with earthly kingdoms. It originated from a different place and will find its destiny in another place. The kingdom of God will only rule over the nations of the earth when Jesus returns. In our day the kingdom of God is never to be merged with any political system on earth.

That doesn't mean that Christians cannot be involved in politics, they can and must, and as citizens we must vote. Such individuals can influence the decisions of government. However, they cannot create a Christian state. Simply because Christianity cannot be imposed by law. If Christian activity is not performed as an outflow of the heart, it is worthless.

Jesus illustrated this principle in a parable. (Matt 13:24-30)

"The kingdom of heaven is like a man who sowed good seed in his field. But while everyone was sleeping, his

enemy came and sowed weeds among the wheat, and went away. When the wheat sprouted and formed heads, then the weeds also appeared. The owner's servants came to him and said, 'Sir, didn't you sow good seed in your field? Where then did the weeds come from?' An enemy did this,' he replied. The servants asked him, 'Do you want us to go and pull them up?' 'No,' he answered, 'because while you are pulling the weeds, you may uproot the wheat with them. Let both grow together until the harvest. At that time, I will tell the harvesters: First collect the weeds and tie them in bundles to be burned; then gather the wheat and bring it into my barn.'

This passage reveals the enormous flexibility in Christianity. It can operate in democracies where government policy reflects public opinion. It can operate in a dictatorship where government policy is imposed by a single person with great power. It may be ostracised, compromised, or even persecuted but it can still exist because it is seated in the hearts of believers.

To believe in Jesus is to live in a parallel kingdom. Jesus lived in a parallel kingdom. Governments may pass anti-biblical laws and people will take advantage of it. Jesus said this would be the case. We don't have to do it. We can still choose to live by our belief in Jesus.

Several of the disciples had thought that to live in the Kingdom of God, the people of Israel had to be liberated from Rome. Judas was one, Peter another. They even questioned him about it at the ascension. *'Are you at this time going to restore the kingdom to Israel.' Acts 1:6.*

There will be a day when the promises to Abraham will be fulfilled and Jesus will reign in a political as well as a spiritual kingdom when he returns. But the gospel needs no such kingdom in which to exist. Go into all the world. It doesn't matter what system of government you encounter, present the gospel. Pray for the governments, seek to influence the governments, obey the governments, but never seek to become the government. In the end we see in the book of Revelation that there will be people from every nation, tribe, people and language in heaven.

.

Truth.

Jesus concludes his remarks, *'I came into the world to testify to truth. Everyone on the side of truth listens to me.'*

Jesus' kingdom would not be concerned with armies, finances, buildings, and political systems, it was concerned with truth. What God has to say about the state of humanity and how he intends to deal with it.

What is truth?

Much has been made of Pilate's question. I believe his question to be a deadly serious inquiry. Not 'truth' in a spiritual sense, but truth in a practical sense. Who was telling the truth in this case? As we progress through this trial, we can see Pilate's attitude changing. He started off with a sense of 'Let's get this nuisance out of the way' to a consciousness that he was dealing with something beyond his comprehension.

He tries to release Jesus. The Jewish leaders will not have it. The events unfold.

Pilate decides to flog him and then let him go so he has conferred some punishment, but they won't have that either.

They conflate the Religious and the Civil charges. They argue that to release this 'king' is to challenge the authority of Caesar.

Pilate is scared.

He questions Jesus again. But Jesus does not answer.

Pilate in frustration says, 'do you not know I have the power to put you to death?'

Jesus then said, *'You have no power that has not been granted you from above.'* Neither have the people shouting for my blood outside. Little did they realise that in 30 or so years' time, they would lie mutilated on the streets of Jerusalem themselves, slain by the soldiers of the empire they pledged allegiance to on this day.

Once again Jesus affirmed that his death, and the process that would take him there was in the hands of Almighty God, they had become willing participants in the case for 'unbelief' and therefore they would perish.

Behold your king.

There was Jesus, chained, bruised and bleeding, dirty and in pain. He was dressed in the purple robe, crowned with thorns. Pilate was saying look, he is harmless. Look what we have done to him. He is a weak, defeated, and somewhat insane person. I have knocked the delusions out of him. He is to be pitied rather than feared. Let him go and you will hear no more from him. But they wouldn't have that either.

Pilate eventually succumbs to the baying crowd. What was he afraid of? 19:8.

He would be afraid of a riot, even an uprising, they were not uncommon.

He was afraid of his reputation, his career depended on him doing well.

He was afraid of Jesus. He would have been well aware that Jesus possessed super-human powers. As a Roman he was disposed to belief in gods and the supernatural. He had arrested Jesus, he had abused Jesus, he had mocked Jesus. What was Jesus about to do to him?

Matthew 27:19-26. Matthew tells us of a further two things that happened.

Pilate's wife sent him a message. The man is innocent. Have nothing to do with his death.

Pilate publicly washed his hands of the matter, handing over responsibility to the Jewish leaders. This act had a precedent in Jewish law. Deuteronomy 21:1-18. Pilate was making one last attempt to free Jesus by invoking this ancient custom, which implied no one present can be guilty of shedding his blood. He was arguing, surely you do not want the blood of an innocent man on your hands? It was futile. Pilate was guilty of dereliction of duty in letting and innocent man die. The crowd had no scruples, 'Let his blood be on us and our children.'

His death was at the hands of both Jew and Gentile. Pilate had not absolved himself of responsibility as he was still making decisions regarding the Inscription Board. 19:22.

These dark moments illustrate to us the there is no such thing as non-belief; that is, I have not considered the matter. There is no such thing as a-belief; that is, I do not know, or I cannot make up my mind. (agnosticism) The positions are simple to believe or not to believe. And whoever chooses to 'not believe' will surely perish.

4. The Crucifixion. 19:17-18.

There are many gaps in the account of the crucifixion that make some details difficult to understand. This is probably because the early readers of the text would know full well what crucifixion was about and did not need the intricate details.

Golgotha was a place of execution outside of the city walls as they were at the time. The exact site is not proven beyond all doubt, but the weight of archaeological evidence points to the site now occupied by the Church of the Holy Sepulchre. [34]

The area was also a burial site.

The Place.
It was not a pleasant place. It was not 'a green hill far away' as the hymnwriter describes it. It was a rocky outcrop of limestone. Neither was it a hill. It was an escarpment caused by quarrying. It was on a busy thoroughfare where people

---

[34] **Biblical Archaeological Society.**

passed closely by. Matthew 27:38. People were close enough to be able to read the inscription. John 19:20.

There were different forms of the 'cross' used, from a simple upright stake, a 'T' shaped structure, and 'X' shaped structure and the traditional cross image we have become accustomed to. Sometimes the victims were impaled upside down. The weight of archaeological evidence indicates that the cross of Jesus consisted of an upright stake that was fixed in the ground. Then there was a cross beam that was carried by the victim to the execution sight. The victim would have been impaled to the cross beam on the ground and then hoisted up to an attachment on the upright stake. The feet would have then been impaled on the upright stake. There was usually an inscription board that described the crime that the person had committed. Which, when the person was impaled, was hung on the cross.

The cross did not lift the victim up very high from the ground. The soldier who pierced his side was able to do so from the ground. But high enough that the sponge of vinegar needed to be fixed to a stick to reach the mouth.

Strangely, Crucifixion was not primarily a method of execution. It was first of all a method of torture. This can be seen by the fact that death was brought about by breaking the legs of the victim, not the crucifixion itself. 19:32. This meant the victim could no longer raise the body to breathe and so they suffocated. The text seems to indicate some surprise when they found Jesus already dead.

Who carried the cross? Matthew, Mark and Luke clearly say that it was carried by Simon of Cyrene. John contradicts this by saying Jesus carried his own cross. 19:16. Traditionally it has been said that Jesus started out carrying his cross but fell under the burden and Simon was forced to carry it for him. There is nothing in any of the gospels to suggest this happened. It was just a way of reconciling John and the synoptics.

To say that Jesus was weakened by the abuse and flogging so that he could not carry the cross all the way does not consider that all crucifixion victims were flogged before being crucified, yet they usually carried the cross beam. [35]

A careful reading of the text seems to show that Simon was compelled to carry the beam from the judgement hall. John says that by the time they came to Golgotha, Jesus was carrying the cross. We don't know where things changed but the gate of the city would be a possible place. The reason could have been that the Romans thought it better not to let a Jew carry his cross in the city during the Passover in case it fermented further trouble. But once out of the city the usual procedure of the victim carrying his own cross was resorted to.

There are few words better arranged than these to describe the day of the crucifixion than these by Getty and Townend.

'Oh to see the pain
Written on Your face
Bearing the awesome weight of sin'

It would never have crossed the minds of those people, long ago, as they witnessed this event, that for 2000 years people have poured over their every word and action trying to reconstruct those sacred steps. They were witnessing the final enactment of what every sacrifice and ceremony ever made had sought to describe.

The Inscription. 19:19-22.

The purpose of the inscription board was to identify the crime of the person being crucified. It was worn around the neck of the person from the place of judgement to the place of

---

[35] **Josephus. Jewish Wars 5:11**

execution. It was supposed to be a deterrent to those watching and it was to bring shame, embarrassment, guilt and exposure on the victim. Of course, with Jesus the stigma of shame became a badge of honour.

It was written in three languages, Hebrew, Greek and Latin. [36] It said;

this is Jesus King of the Jews.	Matthew
The King of the Jews.	Mark
This is the King of the Jews.	Luke
Jesus of Nazareth, the King of the Jews.	John

We can see that they all said, 'this is the King of the Jews' so we can be certain of that. We can also be sure that there was a personal identification. So, we can say that Mark and Luke abbreviated what they saw. As Jesus was a common name, it would also seem probable that the words, *'Jesus of Nazareth'* were used.

This was intended to insult, humiliate, and mortify the person concerned. The gospel has an amazing way of taking that which meant for your harm and turning into good.

Think of the appendages attached to people of faith in scripture. Rahab the harlot; Simon the leper; Mary from whom he had cast seven devils, Paul the persecutor, and so on. These definitions reveal the Grace of God. These appendages no longer bring shame but portray the triumph of Grace. They thought they were describing who he thought he was but failed to be. In fact, Jesus' earthly ministry came to an end with the prophecy of who he would be when he comes again. As the use of the three languages indicates, his kingship on that day would not be confined to the borders of

---

[36] There is such a board in the Church of Santa Croce in Gerusalemme in the city of Rome. Its authenticity is disputed but there is also compelling evidence in its favour. The Quest for the True cross. Thiede and Dancona

Israel, but his kingdom would stretch from shore to shore. Pilate at last had found some courage not to be swayed any further.

The garment. 19:23-24.

Whatever Jesus was wearing the items could be divided into five things. The soldiers divided up his garments in to four parts, suggesting there were four soldiers present. The fact that the soldiers bothered to do this only reflects on their economic paucity. What would they want with the blood-stained clothes of a crucified man?

It meant of course that Jesus was now reduced to utmost ignominy of hanging naked on the cross.

Then there was the seamless robe. This could well be the 'Tallit, the *tassled* garment' which every Jewish man was compelled to wear. Numbers 15:37-41.

What they did was in fulfilment of the scriptures from Psalm 22:18. They decided not to tear it but cast lots for it. Being woven, it would have simply unravelled. Maybe that was it, the thread would have used to make something else.

When Jesus fulfilled the scripture by entering into Jerusalem on the foal of a donkey, it was not a miraculous thing. He arranged it in order to fulfil the scriptures. But here we have 4 men who do not know the scriptures and did not know they were fulfilling scripture, nevertheless they were doing just that. The word of God will not fail. The promises of God will be upheld. The prophecies of scripture will come to pass. Sometimes those things will be in the hands of men of Faith, and at other times they will be in the hands of men of no Faith. As we approach the return of our Lord, some of the preparation is being done by people of Faith. Those who know the scriptures should live in fulfilment of the scriptures. But godless people of no faith are also making decisions that will lead the world to the same destiny, the return of Christ.

It reveals to us the ongoing sovereignty of the King of Kings and the Lord of Lords.

The people

John takes care to point out to us who was at the cross, and by the same token, who was not there.

His mother. His mother's sister, Mary the wife of Clopas, Mary Magdalene, and John. The obscurity of the second woman is probably John's device of not naming himself or people close to him. It has been strongly suggested it was Salome, John's own mother. This would make John and James cousins of Jesus.

In protestant, and especially evangelical circles, we have tended to reduce the role of Mary the mother of Jesus to that of simply bringing the Christ into the world. This is of course in opposition to the Orthodox position that tends to give her much prominence.

At this moment Mary was walking through the fulfilment of a prophecy given to her when the child was born. *'A sword will pierce your own soul too.'* Luke 2:35. She would be 'The Mother of Sorrows.' [37] By now Mary would have been about 50 years of age.

Here at the moment of his own death he makes provision for her welfare. It indicates that Joseph was no longer around. But what of the 'brothers and sisters' of Jesus, didn't they have an obligation to their mother? Matthew 13:55-56. It seems that at this stage they did not believe in him. 7:3-5.

Mary's sorrow was not her own fault. She was who she was because God had chosen her to be the mother of the Christ-child. Jesus recognised her predicament was because of him, he was responsible, so the Saviour took care of her. In this he

---

[37] **Pulpit Commentary.**

created a new family. He had said earlier *'whoever does God's will is my brother and sister and mother.' Mark 3:31-35.* The sword will pierce you **also**. The sword will pierce the Saviour, the Saviour's Mother, and all who would believe on him; therefore, you need to take care of one another. This is the new commandment. 13:34. The world will hate us just as it has hated our Saviour 15:18. When the sword pierces the heart of a brother or sister in Christ then we are to take action to care for them.

5. Two more sayings from the cross. 19: 28-30.

When we compare the gospels, we see that there were seven sayings from the cross. John only records three.

I am thirsty. Jesus is the one who had said, 'If anyone drinks of the water I shall give him, he will never thirst again.' And also, 'Let him who is thirsty come unto me and drink.'

The text says that Jesus knew that everything had been done on the earthly side of the atonement for sin. We are fulfilling the final scriptures. Psalm 69; 3,21. He was now to pass into another realm where the battle would continue on another level.

His cry was no doubt a physical thing but like everything taking place was full of symbolism, which when the apostles gave it thought, blossomed into the truth of the Atonement.

Wine and Hyssop. Let me repeat, we have men who knew nothing, and cared nothing for the scriptures, or who Jesus claimed to be, fulfilling the symbolism of the scriptures.

Wine represents blood. Hyssop, because of its medicinal properties, signified cleansing and purification.

The first time we see the two things together is in Exodus 12:22.

Then at the ceremony of the cleansing of a leper. Leviticus 14:1-7.

Cleansing after coming into contact with a dead body. Numbers 19.

Then the prayer of David. Psalm 51:6-10.

'Cleanse me with hyssop and I will be clean.' That is a cleansing within, the gift of a pure heart.

To put these things together the hyssop and the wine signified the perfect sacrifice, without spot or blemish, Jesus the sinless Saviour. As the perfect sacrifice Jesus will be able to cleanse and save all who come to God by him, so granting a perfect salvation against which there is no condemnation. The symbolism of Numbers 19 is that the ashes of the heifer were able to cleanse and purify the repentant sinner as long as they lasted, because the animal was pure. The blood of Jesus is an eternal sacrifice and is available to anyone who calls on his name.

Hebrews 9:11-15. *'How much more will the Blood of Christ cleanse our consciences from acts that leads to death?'*

> *Bearing shame and scoffing rude*
> *In my place condemned he stood*
> *Sealed my pardon with his blood,*
> *Hallelujah what a Saviour* [38].

It is finished. The Greek word is 'Tetelestai.' It means everything is now fulfilled and complete. The mission is perfectly fulfilled in every detail. That which has been accomplished is now in force and its benefits can be experienced. A new era has begun. A debt has been paid.

He finally yields up his life. Not to cease to exist but to enter into a spiritual war wherein he will make an open show of the powers of hell, much as they had made an open show of him on the cross. But as they had failed, he does not fail, for he will rise from the dead. From now on, he who believes can

---

[38] **Philip Bliss. Redemption Hymnal**

break the shackles of guilt and shame and pass through the bars of sin into a life righteousness and holiness.

6. The piercing. 19:34.

This again is the act of a godless man fulfilling the word of God. None of his bones shall be broken and he will be pierced. Psalm 34:20; Zechariah 12:10. Was this the soldier who Luke tells us said, *'Surely this was a righteous man.'* Luke 23:47. It cannot be put better than in the words of the Prince of Poets, William Cowper.

> *There is a fountain filled with blood,*
> *Drawn from Immanuel's veins,*
> *And sinners plunged beneath that flood*
> *Lose all their guilty stains:*
> *The dying thief rejoiced to see*
> *That fountain in His day;*
> *And there have I, though vile as he,*
> *Washed all my sins away.*
> *Dear dying Lamb, Thy precious blood*
> *Shall never lose its power,*
> *'Till all the ransomed church of God*
> *Are safe, to sin no more:*
> *Ever since by faith I saw the stream*
> *Thy flowing wounds supply,*
> *Redeeming love has been my theme,*
> *And shall be till I die:* [39]

Indeed, were it not for this brief snippet of information our hymn books and prayer books would be very thin indeed. Water and blood flowed from the Saviour's side. I am not so concerned here with the medical explanation of what

---

[39] **William Cowper. Redemption Hymnal.**

happened but the spiritual significance. The death of Christ forgives and cleanses. 1 John1:9. *'If we confess our sins, he is faithful and just, and will forgive us our sins and cleanse us from all unrighteousness.*

Let the water and the blood,
From Thy riven side which flowed,
Be of sin the double cure,
Cleanse me from its guilt and power. [40]

So moved is John by writing these words, and overwhelmed by what they mean, he gives us what amounts to a sacred oath, that what he has written is a true account of what he saw. 19:35. The picture is, as the blood flowed to the earth, the people of the world were embraced in the love of God, and a new covenant was made with the people of the earth. Those that believed would receive eternal life, those that had yet not believed, had the opportunity to believe and pass from death to life.

7. The Burial 19:38-42.

We have finally arrived at the final step. We come to Joseph's tomb. It was a cave like structure carved into the rock as was common for people of substance at the time. It would be a family tomb, intended to take care of several generations. It would consist of a rock hewn table to prepare the bodies for internment. The bodies would be laid on shelves, cut in the rock, until they decomposed. Decomposition took a few weeks. Then the bones would be collected and placed in an ossuary (a box for storing bones) the shelf would then be ready for the next family member who would pass away. The tombs would be visited many times and so access was through a small aperture which was sealed with a moveable stone. Sometimes these stones were rounded to make

---

[40] **A M Toplady. Redemption Hymnal**

access easier. It seems Joseph's tomb had a round stone. Luke 24:1

We are told that Joseph is a secret believer. He gets permission to bury the body. Permission was necessary because crucified people are not usually buried. Often, it seems, they were cremated in the fire in the Hinnom valley. Pilate is still involved in the procedure despite having washed his hands of the matter. Strangely the people who accompanied Jesus while he was alive have gone, and those who were reluctant to be identified with him now come onto the scene. It seems clear that their motives were to end the ignominy and shame, give him a decent burial, draw a respectful line under the whole affair and move on.

They bought too many spices to suggest they hoped for a resurrection. They intended to fulfil all the customary arrangements, but they did not have time to complete all the rituals because of the nearness of the Sabbath. His body was not completely embalmed or washed. But they did what they could in the time they had. The body was loosely wrapped and the head cloth or 'sudarium' that had covered his head was laid in a separate place. [41]It seems that it was arranged that the women would come after the sabbath to complete the job and that the disciples had a report of what was done. Mark 15:47 What they did not allow for of course, was the fact that Pilate would place a guard on the tomb and seal it. However, as it transpired none of this was to be important.

The earthly journey of the Saviour was complete, from the virgin womb to the virgin tomb. The same Holy Spirit that overshadowed the womb would also overshadow the tomb. A miraculous conception would become a miraculous

---

[41] There is a shroud kept in the Cathedral of Turin that some claim to be this actual shroud. It is disputed but there remains compelling evidence. There is also a sudarium in the Cathedral of Oviedo in Spain that some claim to be the 'head cloth' of Jesus. It is disputed but there is compelling evidence. The Quest for the true cross. Thiede and Dancona.

resurrection. Angels attended his birth, angels attended his resurrection

We see that it was clearly established that Jesus was dead. This is important for there are those who still say that Jesus only was unconscious, and aroused in the coolness of the tomb. It is also important that it was an unused tomb. When Jesus arose, there could be no confusion that it was he.

Many commentators are critical of these two men, shaming them for their secrecy. I hear what is being said, but were it not for these men the burial would not have taken place with dignity, if at all. Joseph was able to do it because he could afford to do so, somehow, he had the ear of Pilate, and he was not under suspicion of ulterior motives. Let us not judge people who have to live in complex circumstances. We have no idea of the pressure these men lived under, and why, in their wisdom, it was best not to make their faith obvious until this moment.

Isaiah's words have now come to pass, *'he was assigned a grave with the wicked and with the rich in his death.'* Isaiah 53:9. This, I believe can be best understood as, *"They gave him a grave among criminals, but he ended up instead in a rich man's tomb although he had done no violence nor spoken deceitfully.' Passion Translation.* However, it is to be admitted this does stretch the strict Hebrew translation somewhat which prefers that *'the wicked and the rich'* are a composite clause. The problem we have with it is, that had Jesus been interred with the criminals, it would have been wicked but not rich, and as it turned out, Joseph was rich but not wicked. Maybe the Passion translation has grasped the dynamics of the words.

THE EPILOGUE

John went on to become the third most proliferent writer in the NT behind Luke and Paul respectively. John was the only one of the original twelve to live throughout the Apostolic Age. He was one of the first to believe. He was present on the Mount of Transfiguration when the disciples had a glimpse of the Coming Kingdom; he was the only man to be present at the cross; he was present at the ascension; he was present on the day of Pentecost; he was present when the first miracle of the Apostolic age occurred. (Acts 3:6) John was sent with Peter to pray that the Samaritans receive the Holy Spirit (Acts 8:14) John was bereaved of his brother James. (Acts 12:2) John was one of the leaders who authenticated Paul as a valid minister of the gospel. As the apostles died, usually by execution, John became the only survivor. As such he was highly revered and respected. He became the final authority on what Jesus had said and done.

A timeline. [42]

It is not possible to be absolutely certain of the progress of events in John's life as the evidence is insufficient. However, we can sketch an outline of probability.

---

[42] **New Testament Times; New Testament Survey Tenney.**

The encounter with Paul in Galatians 2:9 is reliably dated at 53. Apparently, John was still based at Jerusalem at this time some 20 years after the crucifixion. We have noted his visit to Samaria but whether he went anywhere else in that period we do not know. Paul lived in Ephesus from 54-57 and was executed in Rome in 68. It seems from this time, according to the Church Fathers, John moved to Ephesus. He seems to have been there for about 20 years before being exiled to Patmos by Emperor Domitian. He was set free by Emperor Nerva. He returned to Ephesus in about 94 where he wrote the letters that bear his name and published the book of Revelation he had written while in exile. He may have lived until the late 90's.

References by the Apostolic Fathers.

The term 'Apostolic Fathers' is a title given to the generation of leaders who became prominent in the second century Their writings are important because they were the disciples of the eyewitnesses. What we learn from them is how they interpreted and applied the teachings they had received from the eyewitnesses. Almost all of the significant Christian leaders of the early second century claim a spiritual heritage from John, either directly as his students, or indirectly as students of students.
They include;
Papias 60-135 Bishop of Hierapolis who claims to have learned from John.
Ignatius of Antioch 35-117 who also claims to have learned from John.
Irenaeus 120-202 was born in Smyrna. He received teaching from Ignatius, Papias and most significantly Polycarp. He is the source of the generally accepted timeline of John's life and ministry.
Clement of Alexandria 150-215. He tells us the motivation for the writing of the gospel of John was to provide a

theological interpretation of the implication of the words of Jesus.

Polycarp 80-167 Smyrna. He claims to have been a disciple and student of John.

Eusebius of Caesarea 260-340. Eusebius tells us that John was familiar with the other gospels but believed that John's gospel 'should be read first of all.' He also confirms the account of John's exile to Patmos. By the end of the 2nd century John's gospel was read throughout the Christian world.

The Beginning.

In his later years John writes what we know today as the Letters of John. He begins with a reference to the 'beginning.' This 'beginning' is not the 'beginning' that is used in the opening verse of John's Gospel. That beginning is the same as the Genesis beginning. Now he is referring to the beginning of the gospel as it was witnessed on earth. John is in effect saying, 'I was there when Jesus began to preach. There was nothing that Jesus said or did that I did not witness. I was there from the beginning to the end of his earthly ministry. I heard what he said and questioned him about what it meant. When it comes to who is telling the truth, there is none more qualified than I.'

- We have seen with our own eyes the things we are telling you about.
- We have heard with our own ears the message we are telling you.
- We have touched him and can testify he was not a ghost or apparition but had human form as we do.
- Jesus appeared and we saw him
- Jesus came from the Father and we witnessed the power and glory of the 'eternal life' he possessed.

John was saying that his readers could believe it or not believe it; but they could not add to it or take away from it and still consider themselves true believers. Once again fellowship with the believers was only extended to those who would likewise confess Jesus as the Son of God.

It seems John's main purpose in writing is to appeal to those who have believed to hold on and remain in the truth and not be led astray. John appeals to the 'beginning' as the source of his authority.

John continues to use words or phrases that were first penned in the gospel. Indicating to us that what we presumed is true, he constantly told and retold the stories of his journey with Jesus.
We find the following amongst others; 'Word, Life, Light, walking in light; walking in darkness; complete joy; obey his commands; love one another; this is how God showed his love for us; eternal life; and the world under the control of the evil one.'

We can see that John has adopted the 'no nonsense' attitude of Jesus himself in his dealings with the Jewish leaders. They believe or not believe; they are children of God or children of the Devil; they obey or disobey and so on. Now John spoke of those who belong and those who never really belonged; the Christ and the antichrists; lovers of the world and the lovers of God; the spirit that recognises that Jesus came in the flesh and the spirit that does not.

The God who is love.

What we know about the nature of God is derived to a great extent from John's insights into the words of Jesus. 1 John 4:7-21.
We understand from John that the Father, Son and Holy Spirit are a unique unity who share a common identity. Sometimes

they are mentioned individually, sometimes just two are mentioned, but never more than these three. We learn they are bound together with a unique quality of love that circulates between them. Each one seeks to honour and promote the other and the particular work they do. So majestic is this relationship that John says plainly, 'God is Love.' That does not mean that God loves everything and everyone the same. That is a description of how God exists and how the Father, Son and Holy Spirit are one.

Then there is the command for believers to love each other in the same way. As Father, Son and Spirit are bound as one in love, so should believers be bound together. Believers should display this love so that it becomes the hallmark of any Christian Community. Again, this is a unique love that is only shared amongst those who believe.

John concludes that there is to be a love that is shared between believer and God. In fact, one cannot claim to love God unless this love for the fellow believer is manifest. This is where God extends his special love that had existed only among Father Son and Spirit to include those who believe. He comes to make his home with us.

Love for the world. The essential nature of God is pure, sacrificial, transparent love. The essential nature of humanity apart from God is 'cravings, lusts, and boastings' (1 John 2:16) As far as John is concerned, we love the world or we love God, the two are incompatible. The word 'world' here is clearly the world systems and philosophies and the people who propagate them. John tells us explicitly, do not love the this 'world.' That is, what the world has become in its state of estrangement from God.

However, as we have said, there is a way in which God does love the world. We are also called to love the world within the same parameters. This 'world' refers to the people of the world. God showed his love for the people of the world in sending Jesus to die for the sin of the world so that all people may be free to believe.

In John's mind, those who refuse to believe are not enveloped in the Love of God. They may benefit from Divine Favour because they are in the proximity of believers, but they do not experience the love within the family of God. (1 Corinthians 7:14) Believers can be called to lay down their lives if necessary for the Gospel. That is declaring the opportunity God has granted to the world that it may choose to be saved. But the unbeliever does not share in the unique love of God until they become part of the family of God through believing in Jesus as the Son of God and the Saviour of the world. When the believer puts him arms around the unbeliever, he is not saying, 'never mind God understands;' he is saying 'come and be part of the family of God and all the blessings that brings by repentance and faith in the Son of God.'

Those who falter. Enough time had passed by for John to understand the necessity for perseverance. The exuberance and excitement of the first encounter had to be translated into a day-by-day relationship with Jesus.

John recognised that the journey of the individual would not be faultless. 1 John 1:8-10. If we sin, we are to confess our sin. If we do not confess it or refuse to admit it, we are in danger of breaking our relationship with God.

The believer cannot live a life of habitual sinning without any concern for its consequences on the perpetrator or others. 1 John 3:7-10. To be 'born of God' is to have a relationship with God that triggers an alarm when sin is contemplated. It means that something has arisen, like a virus, that is attempting to contaminate the pure love of God. To ignore this 'witness' is to ignore the voice of the Spirit of God. This in turn breaks the love-bond between believer and God, and unless it is dealt with, the person drifts further and further away from God. 1 John 3:19-24.

Christianity to John is a real and dynamic relationship between the believer and God through Jesus Christ. As in all relationships it must be maintained. John's experience has taught him that our relationship with God is a matter of ongoing worship, obedience, fellowship, witness, faith, and a pursuit of Christlikeness.

What we have said does not exhaust the meaning of this gospel but hopefully, I trust, it has added something to the understanding of the text that will inspire the hearts of others to search for more.
John has left behind a sacred legacy, preserved over the centuries so that we may read it and believe that Jesus is the Christ the Son of God, and in believing have life in his name.

> *All Hail! The power of Jesu's Name*
> *Let Angels prostrate fall*
> *Bring forth the royal diadem*
> *And crown him Lord of all.*
> *O that with yonder sacred throng*
> *We at his feet may fall*
> *join in the everlasting song*
> *And crown him Lord of all.* [43]

---

[43] **E Perronet Redemption Hymnal.**

BIBLIOGRAPHY

TITLE	AUTHOR(S)	PUBLISER
John: Gospel of Belief	M C Tenney	Eardmans
New Testament Survey	M C Tenney	Baker
New Testament Times	M C Tenney	Baker
Message of John	B Milne	I.V.P.
Dictionary of NT Theology	ed. C Brown	Paternoster
Barnes notes on the NT	A Barnes.	Kregel
Benson Commentary	J Benson.	Online
Adam Clarke Commentary	A. Clarke	Baker
James Fausset and Brown Commentary	J,F & B	Oliphants
Interlinear Greek Nt.	A Marshall	Bagster
B.A.S. Publications	ed. G Corbett	Laden
Hebrew/ English NT		Society for the Distribution of the Hebrew Scriptures.
Quest for the True Cross	D'Ancona and Theide	Weidefeld Nicholson

New International Version of the Holy Bible
New King James Version of the Holy Bible

ABOUT THE AUTHOR

Pastor Graham Field is a retired Pentecostal minister living in the United Kingdom. He has served in Zimbabwe, South Africa and the U.K.
He has a Diploma of theology from the Theological College of Southern Africa and an Associate of Arts Degree from I.C.I. University. USA.
He has planted and led churches in South Africa and the U.K.
He has served on the Board of the International Christian Embassy Jerusalem.
He has been a lecturer in Biblical Archaeology and Hebraic Studies at The International Bible Training Institute, Burgess Hill. U.K.
He has also worked as a Hospital Chaplain.

Printed in Great Britain
by Amazon

65510389R00129